LORI PAUL

SACRED BREATH

Migizi Publishing

Sacred Breath
by Lori Paul

Print ISBN # 978-1-7359153-0-2

Copyright © 2020 by Lori Paul

Published by Migizi Publishing, LLC

Cover Design by Arpit Mehta

www.mehtacollaborative.com

Edited and Formatted for Publication by Ben Wolf

www.benwolf.com/editing-services

Unless otherwise noted, scriptures are taken from the ESV Global Study Bible®, ESV® Bible. Copyright © 2012 by Crossway. The Holy Bible, English Standard Version® (ESV®). Copyright © 2001 by Crossway.

All other scripture verses taken from other translations are copyrighted to their respective publishers.

Printed in the United States of America.

All rights reserved under International Copyright Law. Contents and/or cover may not be reproduced in whole or in part in any form without the express written consent of the Publisher.

Dedicated to יהוה

CONTENTS

1. A Vision Amidst Vulnerability — 7
2. Coming to Life! — 15
3. Water ∼ Mni Wiconi — 21
4. In His Presence — 31
5. Appearing — 49
6. The Creator Speaks — 63
7. What Words Can Do — 75
8. The Power — 85
9. Relational Prayer — 95
10. Keys to the Kingdom — 109
11. Praying For Others — 127
12. A Journey's Prayers — 143
13. Revealing the Power of Blessing! — 159
14. When It's Up to Us — 177
15. Praising — 189
16. Design — 203
17. Horns of Praise, Power, and Faith — 207
18. Spirit and Life — 217

Acknowledgments — 237
About the Author — 239

CHAPTER ONE
A VISION AMIDST VULNERABILITY

SUDDENLY ABLE TO SEE

Searching.

We know there's something about us—something valuable, something unique, something that sets us apart. We search for a purpose and a place and that ultimate connection of this vision.

You are something so much more, and you know it—more than the whole of yourself. More than the blades of grass or the songs of birds, more than the ripples in the stream. There's a depth in you that can feel like an ocean. You have plans and dreams that span unending thoughts and reach out into a vast universe of wonder.

There is and has been only one *you*.

You are alive.

You have thoughts.

You communicate within yourself and to the life around you.

With that one moment's glimpse of all you have been in search of and hoped for is revealed to you, your deep cries out to the deep. That which was created within you to drive you to search for meaning finally finds the source of that infinite deep.

It is the ultimate connection, purpose, place and the value of who you are with the One whose breath gave you life.

The Creator breathed so that you could have life. With all of your days of the rising of the sun and to its setting, you begin to search to know Him who knew you before your body was formed. He planned and counted those days for you before even one of them came to be. (Psalm 139:16)

This revelation has always dwelled in the midst of so much. It is a fresh day in your life, planned, to know the Giver of Life in the depths of how you are designed. The story of old, to live in the greater understanding of being made in the Creator's image, sets the flow that leads to deeper understanding of the ancient writings of what has been called the Living Word.

By way of His Spirit, the Creator stepped in and made Himself known. He is giving us the things for which we have been hungering and thirsting. May the fullness of Creator/Yahweh/YHVH reveal to you and exhale into you fresh, life-giving breath for you to know how precious you are to Him. How wonderfully you are created.

You are designed for a life of power, grace, love, hope, peace, joy, relationship and great purpose. To life! To live! *L'chayim!*

It was my first book. I'd finished my manuscript and was beginning the process of working through the publishing. I was scared, not just because this was my first book but because this book was opening a door into my private life at that time.

That morning, I prayed earnestly. I sat in the quietest corner of my living room on the sofa we'd bought just before my first child was born. That sofa was now twenty-five years old and still silky white… mostly. There were a few stains here and there, but I had flipped over cushions to hide the worst of them.

My head tipped down, my hands folded in gripped sincerity. With my eyes shut, I saw the most beautiful thing I have ever seen—a vision.

I saw something like a white dove. It flew from a crown, paused in the middle as I looked upon it, and then it flew over to a perfectly shaped outline of a heart. Next to the heart sat another heart with a break in its outline. The heart with the break in it joined the perfect heart through the opening of the break, and then it became whole and linked to the perfect heart, never to be separated.

I recognized the beautiful symbolism as I thought of all of the brokenness in people and our lives. Often this is the place where we can finally see how much we need to be whole. We can't fill the empty place or heal the breaks without something bigger than us, better than us, loving us and forgetting our every wrong.

We can connect to that Savior, that Messiah, the only One who has shown He is who He said He is in fulfilling prophecies and the ultimate love in sacrifice. Yeshua, the one the Greeks called Jesus, asked the soldiers who they wanted. They said to him, "Yeshua of Nazareth." He responded, "I AM he." And with that, the soldiers fell to the ground. (John 18:6)

In the tribal language of the people, "Yeshua" means "Yah Saves," and "Nazareth" means the "Branch." In His power and perfection, Yeshua gives forgiveness, love, and grace when He joins with us. That place of brokenness or emptiness becomes whole.

Yeshua promises that nothing can separate us from His love. We are permanently linked to Him. The hearts are that: love. The crown was to be worn by the King of Kings. From it flew the dove to the hearts that joined, and the broken was made whole.

But that dove-like figure completely took over my thoughts and curiosity, and it inspired the beginning of what would be a year-long journey of study. It was white, and it moved more gracefully and lovely than anything I had ever seen.

Its wings and tail stretched out, and each outstretched feather reached out and contracted independently of the others. Even as the dove figure paused for me to look upon it, the feathers remained busy and ever-moving.

It looked misty like my breath on one of our cold Minnesota days, but it didn't dissipate or thin out and disappear, not even as the wings, tail, and feathers reached out. Neither did it condense and become opaque as they retracted.

It was elegant. It was graceful. It was gorgeous while constantly moving its wings, feathers, and tail as it drifted across my view, following what looked like its head as it went across to the hearts and then disappeared.

It was the most captivating thing I had ever seen. I was releasing a book with prayer from a very vulnerable place, and in that moment, He took my mind off of myself and placed a fresh vision that would begin something completely new. So I went chasing after the dove-like figure.

Grasping for my Bible, I thought about when Jesus/Yeshua was baptized and the Holy Spirit that descended like a dove. I opened to Luke 3:22 KJV and read, "and the *Holy Spirit* descended on him in bodily form *like* a dove. And a voice came from heaven: 'You are my Son, whom I love; with you I am well pleased.'"

It said *like* a dove. It didn't say "as" a dove, but *like* a dove.

I searched some more and found Matthew 3:16-17 (emphasis added):

---

[16]As soon as Jesus was baptized, he went up out of the water. At that moment heaven was opened, and he saw the Spirit of God descending *like* a dove and lighting on him. [17]And a voice from heaven said, "This is my Son, whom I love; with him I am well pleased."

There it was again in Matthew's gospel—*like*.

In Isaiah 42:1, as YHVH gave prophecy and established connections to the New Testament, more was written about the Holy Spirit: "Here is my servant, whom I uphold, my chosen one in whom I delight; I will put my Spirit on him and he will bring justice to the nations." There is a promise here—a prophecy.

Then came the word that put the power behind the vision I had seen during prayer. The word *ruah* is an ancient Hebrew word that means both "breath" and "spirit." It also means "mind" and "wind."

One word meant these things.

One word used numerously throughout the ancient texts of the Bible.

Knowing this adds so much more to Isaiah 11:2: "The Spirit of the LORD will rest on him—the Spirit of wisdom and of understanding, the Spirit of counsel and of power, the Spirit of knowledge and of the fear of the LORD—"

Overcome with this new knowledge, I revered YHVH in holy fear in the ways of His presence and that incredible moment of that gift of "seeing" Him like never before. Discovering the word "Ruah" felt like a window shade being abruptly lifted in a dark room and allowing the sun to shine into my eyes.

Perhaps Luke and Matthew, Jesus' followers and writers of the time, and those witnessing the dove-like form descending didn't know what one's breath looked like. They lived in a warmer climate. They didn't grow up in the winters of Minnesota where the warmth and moisture of our breath is easily and frequently visible against the cold air.

But for me, breath was suddenly thrust into a new focus.

It is something that has always been there: breath. I noticed it in the early days of my Bible reading and recognized its importance in the creation of man, but like my own breath, I stopped thinking about it.

Now awakened with new eyes, I began to think about it more fully. I prayed about it, asking for YHVH's truths, and He captured my every attention as I developed an intense desire to discover more. I researched the physical with the spiritual, because according to the Bible, our human life was started by the Creator's breath.

Looking at our lives now, our first breaths out of the womb come with cheers from those who are helping to deliver us and waiting for that sign of life. Then... the breathing continues. We no longer notice the baby's breath much.

Not even our own.

In our sleep, we breathe. Our heart beats without any of our control. All of our other organs function fully without our ability to control them. But our breath, necessary for life, can be controlled to an extent. Eventually, we must inhale. This isn't because our lungs need it; it is because our blood must have oxygen and expunge carbon dioxide.

The way we can see breath is in the *exhale*, like on a cold day. When the Creator breathed into Adam, it was an *exhale*. How beautiful! The Creator's very breath, purposely given for our *life*. Genesis 2:7 reads, "then, YHVH formed the man from the dust of the ground and breathed into his nostrils the breath of life, and the man became a living being."

From the Creator came life, soul, and our mind created by His breath. This is the most intimate act of creation, with His own hands forming us and the nearness: the Creator breathes into our very nostrils with His Life and Spirit.

We are formed by His own hands; we are created in His image in more than body. He breathed an eternity of soul and thought, emotions capable of hope, peace, and love, igniting our spirits with life. But because of Adam's sin, death became part of this life.

In the New Testament, Yeshua is described as the last Adam. He is the one who did not sin and *restored* what was lost.

2 Corinthians 15:45 reads, (emphasis added) "So it is written: 'The first man Adam became a living being.'" The last Adam, a life-giving spirit. And Job 33:4 reads, "The Spirit of God has made me; the breath of the Almighty gives me life."

We don't think much about breathing.

Think about the Creator breathing.

The entire Bible is considered God-breathed. "All Scripture is *God-breathed* and is useful for teaching, rebuking, correcting and training in righteousness, 17 so that the man of God may be *thoroughly equipped for every good work.*" (2 Timothy 3:16, emphasis added)

On BibleHub.com, the Barnes Commentary says this about 2 Timothy 3:16-17 of scripture being God-breathed:

Is given by inspiration of God - All this is expressed in the original by one word - Θεόπνευστος Theopneustos. This word occurs nowhere else in the New Testament. It properly means, God-inspired - from Θεός Theos, "God," and πνέω pneō, "to breathe, to breathe out." The idea of "breathing upon, or breathing into the soul," is that which the word naturally conveys. Thus, God breathed into the nostrils of Adam the breath of life Genesis 2:7, and thus the Savior breathed on his disciples, and said, "receive ye the Holy Ghost;" John 20:22 The idea seems to have been, that the **life was in the breath, and that an intelligent spirit was communicated with the breath.** The expression was used among the Greeks, and a similar one was employed by the Romans.

What YHVH was pointing to was *more* than I had ever studied at length. His prompting by the beautiful sight of His Spirit in the form of a breath-like dove during prayer had led to an understanding of life that was taking on a life of its own.

My dad is a physicist. He is an expert on the study of energy and matter. He worked on many "top secret" projects while I was growing up and has received twenty-seven patents for inventions over the course of his science and research career.

He instilled in me a desire to discover through research what was fueled by curiosity and the joy of discovery and learning. It has suddenly kicked in.

To quote my Mom regarding my recent science passion, "She's a REALLY late bloomer."

I had been made for this, and YHVH led my every curiosity and thought as He revealed what has always been there in His Word. In the physical and the spiritual, He is in and of it all. And as my father worked in the sciences, he said that the more he discovered, the more he saw the Creator, and so grew his faith.

This passage of scripture is *key* to the spiritual part of breath and the spiritual life that is fully given even while in our physical bodies:

> On the evening of that first day of the week, when the disciples were together, with the doors locked for fear of the Jews, Yeshua/Jesus came and stood among them and said, "Peace be with you!" 20After he said this, he showed them his hands and side. The disciples were overjoyed when they saw the Lord. 21 Again Yeshua/Jesus said, "Peace be with you! As the Father has sent me, I am sending you." 22And with that he breathed on them and said, "Receive the Holy Spirit." (John 20:19-22 19)

The breath of Life was released! Death and resurrection now was evidenced in His body as He stood fully and eternally alive breathing out Ruah Ha Kodesh; the Holy Spirit. Calling and purpose had begun.

CHAPTER TWO
COMING TO LIFE!

"I am the way the truth and the life.
No one comes to the Father except through Me."
(John 14:6)

As Yeshua spoke, He laid claim to all life. He gave life through His Spirit and His own blood as our sacrifice. How richly loved we are for Him to be made as man—so loved that He desired our very lives.

We have been created in life and saved for life so that we can be with Him in eternal life.

From the very beginning existed the Tree of Life. "And out of the ground made YHVH to grow every tree that is pleasant to the sight, and good for food; the tree of life also in the midst of the garden, and the tree of knowledge of good and evil." (Genesis 2:9 KJV)

The creation of the *exchange* of what we need and what a tree needs is an incredible thing in itself. Trees produce oxygen and we produce the carbon dioxide that a tree needs to live.

I think of everything that grows, and the color is predominantly green. Carbon dioxide is a byproduct of our spent energy, and then we draw our fuel back from the oxygen of the living trees and plants. The green is everywhere in the growing seasons in Minnesota.

This is not only a physical give-and-take but a symbolic one, too. Think of the way water reflects the heavens. This, too, is a reflection of sorts. We are all connected.

When I think of the Creator and His breath and His exchange with us, I can't help but notice: "And he who sat there had the appearance of jasper and carnelian, and around the throne was a rainbow that had the appearance of an emerald." (Revelation 4:3)

Around Him, from where He sits, glows a rainbow of green—the reflection of Earth and Heaven.

Visualize what a tree looks like, and look at this image. It is an x-ray of the *human bronchial tree* of the trachea and lungs held upside down. Look at the Creator's design in this exchange.

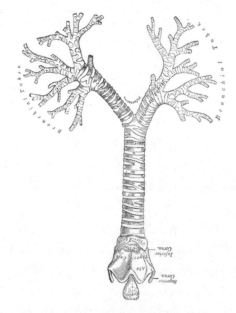

Inverted image of the bronchial tubes of human lungs -
Public Domain Images

Breath, and the exchange of breath, is intimate. It means life between us and the living plants. We feel it in nearness. It comes from deep within. Before a couple's lips meet in a kiss, they feel the breath. It is a unique part of the other person.

Holding a baby close and nuzzling it, the smell of their little downy head and milky mouth as you kiss or rub your cheek on theirs is another example of intimate closeness. You know the fragrance of your child. Holding a child on your lap, you feel the breath and bond; it is a close intimacy.

As a new and nervous mother with a newborn, I often dipped my finger near my sleeping baby to feel their warm breath upon my finger to assure they were well. It comforted me to hold my ear near and listen to the breaths and feel them on my own cheek, and it filled me with an indescribable pleasure. It always brought a smile to my face.

Even as a child rests its head on a parent's chest, the child will listen to the repetition of breathing and sometimes match their own breath with the same timing of the inhale and exhale. There is also recognition that imprints the scent of the dear one. The sense of smell is the strongest sense to trigger memory. (Live Science "Why Do Smells Trigger Strong Memories?" by Yasemin Saplakoglu)

As a young adult, after one of my grandparents passed on, I had pressed my face into the clothing still hanging in their closet. I closed my eyes and breathed in deeply the familiar scent that only they carried, as it comforted me and made me feel near to them once again. Many times, I secretly stepped into that scent-filled closet for comfort.

The Creator breathed into man's nostrils. Yeshua breathed on His disciples and said, "Receive My Spirit." This is intimacy and nearness and life and love as we breathe Him in.

Job is known for his sufferings. There is even more to his suffering when you read Job 19:17: "My breath is strange to my wife, and I am a stench to the children of my own mother."

Job's breath was affected in his suffering. He was not even known to his wife, as he seemed to be "strange" or like someone else, not her husband. His breath was strange to his wife and even smelled wrong to his own brothers and sisters, those who grew up with him and probably knew every possible way he could smell.

The Lord allowed his breath to suffer. This kept him at distance from the ones he held dear. He no longer had the intimacy and closeness that had once carried a fragrance of being known and endeared.

Breath is a part of intimacy.

Breath is a part of our words, and David captured it as prayer, wanting it to be desirable: "May my prayer be set before you like incense; may the lifting up of my hands be like the evening sacrifice." (Psalm 141:2)

I found this and wondered if David's prayer was answered or if it had always been part of Heaven and instead the Holy Spirit had placed that longing in David.

Another verse that draws this together found in the New Testament is Revelation 5:8: "And when he had taken it, the four living creatures and the twenty-four elders fell down before the Lamb. Each one had a harp and they were holding golden bowls full of incense, which are the prayers of the saints."

The bowls held significance as I pictured the weight of the prayers and consistency to be contained in bowls. The words and breaths of prayer were individual and intimate. They were described as being incense held by the elders and surely went down before the Lamb as the elders did: preciously held in golden bowls.

The smoke and breath used in a ceremonial pipe and the bowl that holds the sacred tobacco as prayers are lifted to the Creator have been part of the physical in Native tradition, but the meaning and intimacy is to be representative of the spiritual between the Creator and us.

The pipe symbolizes prayer and relationship. When prayer and relationship happen in the heart, the true Spirit of Yeshua lives within us.

The words mattered. "In the beginning was the Word, and the Word was with God, and the Word was God." (John 1:1)

God Himself *is* the Word, which is God-breathed, and our breathed words back to Him are as important to us in that relationship of a spiritual life. As plants give us life through their exchange and we give back in ours, we are all connected. Our prayers are our connection to our Creator. It is part of the intimate exchange.

Here is where the spiritual and physical started to be noticed in a great degree: *We can only speak on the exhale.* We know this but don't think about it.

Babies experiment with how they make sounds in their babble. They attempt their "dah-dah-dahs" on the inhale, and in their exhale, it becomes loud and carries. Soon they make their voice sounds on the exhale only.

The Word is an exhale. Yahweh's life-giving breath into Adam's nostrils is an exhale. Yeshua breathed on His disciples and said, "Receive My Spirit." One gives that which is within themselves in the exhale.

What is the difference between an exhale and an inhale? I looked up the components:

Inhaled air = 78% nitrogen, 21% oxygen, 0.9% argon, 0.04% carbon dioxide, 0% water

Exhaled air = 75% nitrogen, 16% oxygen, 0.9% argon, 4% carbon dioxide, 4% water

---

Water was the one major ingredient found in an exhale verses an inhale. Our exhaled air is rated at 100% humidity. (users.rowan.edu "Respiration" by Dr. Stephanie Farrell)

The scriptures continued to come alive to me as our physical world and life intertwined with the Word of Yahweh and His Spirit.

CHAPTER THREE
WATER ~ MNI WICONI

WATER IS LIFE

Genesis 1:2 ESV says, "The earth was without form and void, and darkness was over the face of the deep. And the Spirit of God was hovering over the face of the waters."

I had always read the next few verses and passed them by... until now.

Genesis 1:6-8 reads, "6 And God said, "Let there be space between the waters, to separate water from water." 7 And so it was. God made this space to separate the waters above from the waters below. 8 And God called the space "sky." This happened on the second day."

I found an ancient Hebrew drawing of their view of Creation, and the drawing depicted the separation of waters above and below.

Reading this revealed that it had been all water. The Creator created space between the waters and called the space "sky." We weren't all sky and then water. It was water... everywhere.

The Hebrew word for water is "mayim." The Hebrew word for *heaven* is "shamayim." Heaven has the word water in it and can loosely mean, "the waters are there" or "there the waters." Another definition for *shamayim* is, "superlative waters."

The human body is made mostly of water. The Creator's big, beautiful, life-giving breath into dust gave us life. Our scientists search outer space and the planets looking for any signs of life, particularly for signs of water. All that is alive depends on water. We can survive for longer periods of time without food, but without water, we soon perish.

You are created from the very essence of God and Heaven...

Before you begin to think that this is too unusual, I want you to be aware of the verse below. We will come back and visit it more thoroughly as we continue exploring the way you are created. The Creator's continuous use of water amid His presence and the significance of word, prayer, blessing, praise, and life are linked in incredible ways.

> This is He who came by water and blood—Jesus Christ; not only by water, but by water and blood. And it is the Spirit who bears witness, because the Spirit is truth. **7**For there are three that bear witness [b]in heaven: the Father, the Word, and the Holy Spirit; and these three are one. **8**And there are three that bear witness on earth: the Spirit, the water, and the blood; and these three agree as one. 1 John 5:6-8 NKJV

Let's look at the human body. You. The way you are made. As babies, we are 75-80% water. As we age, that percentage decreases. It is why we wrinkle and shrivel. We hold less water.

There are differing numbers, but the average percentage of water in the brain is 75%. Water conducts electricity, and this is important in the operation of our bodies. The electrical potential is shared between the brain neurons through electrochemical transmitters. This electrical process of brain chemistry must be present for any of our "thoughts" to take place. (*Nutrition in Perspective*, Patricia A. Kreutler, Dorice M. Czajka-Narins. Appendix 554-556)

Water is involved in every function of the body that is required for life.

It is all about *water*.

It helps transport nutrients and waste products in and out of cells. It is necessary for all digestive, absorption, circulatory, and excretion functions. It also helps with the maintenance of proper body temperature. (*Water: The Science of Nature's Most Important Nutrient,* by Len Kravitz, Ph.D)

When someone is dehydrated, they are unable to regulate their temperature, which results in both high fevers and abnormally low temperatures. We experienced this in a great degree as my father-in-law neared death. He would suddenly spike high fevers and then shortly later be cool to the touch and then back to hot without any predictability. Keeping him hydrated help moderate this.

Our lungs are almost 90% water, and their job is to provide oxygen to the blood and remove carbon dioxide. The percentage of water in the organ of the lung surprised me when I first learned about it. I associated lungs with air and had never imagined that large amount of water was making up our lungs.

Every inhale and exhale filters in and out of us through lungs made of 90% water. It's why we can see our breath in the cold and why balloons we blow up are warm and maybe have moisture inside. That isn't just from your mouth—the moisture comes from our lungs.

When we are conceived, within twelve days of conception we are encased in fresh water. This is before the woman even knows she is pregnant and before her time of shedding blood during her moon or menstrual cycle.

The new life forms within a beautiful, transparent case full of fresh water. The evidence of the blood in a menstrual cycle is that no new life has taken hold inside, and the cycle begins again to make ready the ability for life.

When in the womb, the child is in this water, medically known as amniotic fluid. Amniotic fluid is made up of pure water with only 2% salt. Its presence is necessary so it *cushions* and gives *stability* to the child as it grows and its body forms and functions. It also helps protect the baby from disease.

Part of the forming and function is that the *fetus*, which means *young one* in Latin, begins to swallow the water and take "breaths". The inhaled and exhaled breaths of water help strengthen the lungs so that when it is born it has the ability to breathe in air. Our first breath actions are water-filled.

Inside the womb, the baby also swallows water which passes through functioning kidneys. It is part of the development of the kidneys to begin to process this. The child then expels the water as urine. This is when the water becomes other components from the child; the urine and skin cells that have come off become part of the amniotic fluid.

When there is a lack of amniotic fluid, it is a concern and sign for doctors that the lungs and kidneys will not or are not developing properly. The amniotic fluid circulates and flows, and if there is a lack of circulation, webbed fingers and toes can occur, too. (*Medical News Today* "What's to Know about Amniotic Fluid" *Healthline* "How to Increase Amniotic Fluid" Brian Gorton Lecturer in Nursing)

When the water *breaks* the child is *delivered*.

The ability of water to disassemble and rearrange other molecules is *essential to the chemistry of life*. It does this by forming weak bonds with the other molecules. This is often why we refer to water as the *universal solvent.* (*Nutrition in Perspective,* Patricia A. Kreutler, Dorice M. Czajka-Narins. Appendix 554-556)

Another percentage of water loss that impacts our need for water intake is through our respiration. We lose water out from our *breath.* (UTMD Health "Fluid and Electrolyte Therapy")

There is something here. What is it in our breath? The Creator spoke the world into existence. He says that in the beginning was the Word and the Word was with God and the Word was God. (John 1:1)

In Ezekiel 37:1-14, YHVH speaks to Ezekiel. He tells Ezekiel to *speak* to the dry bones. Note that the word "dry" is used. We need to pick up on this.

The hand of YHVH was on me, and he brought me out by the Spirit of YHVH and set me in the middle of a valley; it was full of bones. ² He led me back and forth among them, and I saw a great many bones on the floor of the valley, bones that were very dry. ³ He asked me, "Son of man, can these bones live?"

I said, "Sovereign YHVH you alone know."

⁴ Then he said to me, "Prophesy to these bones and say to them, 'Dry bones, hear the word of YHVH! ⁵ This is what the Sovereign YHVH says to these bones: I will make breath enter you, and you will come to life. ⁶ I will attach tendons to you and make flesh come upon you and cover you with skin; I will put breath in you, and you will come to life. Then you will know that I am YHVH.'"

⁷ So I prophesied as I was commanded. And as I was prophesying, there was a noise, a rattling sound, and the bones came together, bone to bone. ⁸ I looked, and tendons and flesh appeared on them and skin covered them, but there was no breath in them.

⁹ Then he said to me, "Prophesy to the breath; prophesy, son of man, and say to it, 'This is what the Sovereign YHVH says: Come, breath, from the four winds and breathe into these slain, that they may live.'" ¹⁰ So I prophesied as he commanded me, and breath entered them; they came to life and stood up on their feet – a vast army. (Ezekiel 37:1-10)

(*Note: YHVH *is most often pronounced as Yahweh. In the Hebrew translation His Name is used and I have inserted it here.*)

As you read this passage, you see the power of YHVH's Word and the words spoken by Ezekiel. YHVH tells him to *prophecy*. Simply put, prophecy is saying what YHVH said.

This is where it gets fascinating: The word for "prophet" comes from the Hebrew term *niv sefatayim*, meaning "fruit of the lips." Proverbs 15:4 says, "A wholesome tongue is a tree of life, but perverseness in it breaks the spirit."

See the ending of *ayim* in the word "prophet?" We see the partial word for "water" in *mayim*, "Heaven" in *shamayim*, and "prophet" in *niv sefatayim*. We see the waters in Hebrew.

You have been given the capacity to produce fruit from your lips. Picture the bronchial tree again. The tongue can be a part of a tree of life within us and produce fruit from the breath of the words we say.

The spirit is part of our breath just as the one word, *ruah*, means both. To speak perverseness breaks the spirit. It is not life-giving fruit. Prophets are those who speak by the Holy Spirit.

YHVH further commanded Ezekiel to *prophesy to the breath*, and it came from the four winds. YHVH's presence is everywhere. It makes sense that the winds/breath would not come from just one direction, but all. His Spirit, ruah, came in a physical sensation of wind or breath so that they may live in the four directions. The Creator's instruction of worship is seen in the Hebrew like traditional Native ways, recognizing the four directions.

This is also hope to continue in prayer. Even when all looks dead and dry, YHVH can still breathe life into any situation, to restore and bring back. This is an example of His Word being spoken by man. A wholesome tongue is a tree of life!

Psalm 1:3: "He is like a tree planted by streams of water, which yields its fruit in season and whose leaf does not wither. Whatever he does prospers."

Jeremiah 17:8: "He will be like a tree planted by the water that sends out its roots by the stream. It does not fear when heat comes; its leaves are always green. It has no worries in a year of drought and never fails to bear fruit."

A friend recently showed me this photo of a side cut of a blade of grass that has been posted in many social network sites. The blade was dyed so that as to show the channels inside it that take up water and deliver it to the rest of the blade.

Every blade of grass has this within it. Look at what the Creator is revealing to us at this time in life! We are blessed to be alive at this time to be able to see such things with technology.

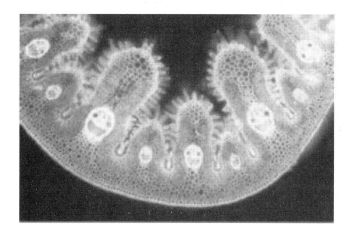

The magnitude of life in science comes together in physical ways that are inescapably linked to the spiritual when you recognize it in YHVH's Word. We are living in an incredible time to have access to science that shows more of His hand and design in both the physical and spiritual.

When I started to see these things and recognize their connections, I never felt more connected to YHVH or more loved or more blessed by Him. All of these pieces to a puzzle started to form a beautiful image. We are created in His image.

Our understanding our Earth and its life has developed in leaps and bounds over the last thirty years. Much of this is thanks to NASA placing satellites in orbit around our Earth which capture stunning images of the planet.

We see the vapors of water in our skies as they swirl in constant motion, birthed and flowing to the waters of the Earth, to the land, to the depths of the seas and life within and above, and the billows of clouds, dust, and lightning strikes. Even the continent of Antarctica pours life out from its perfect cycle of freezing and thawing. Earth is ever-moving and breathing.

All of it speaks life.

Living things also have energy. Photosynthesis and respiration = energy and life. Energy is found in light (*phos* is Greek for light), electricity, sound, heat, and movement. Our thoughts move upon electronic impulses. Our heart beats with its own electrical stimulus. Water is a conductor of electricity. Water is at the basis of it all.

Water is not only essentially important in human life but it is also the life-carrier on Earth. Water vapor connects with life on Earth. Even the desert sands of the Sahara become a fuel for life when mixed with water. In *Earth From Space*. NOVA Online. PBS Video Feb. 2013 it revealed the following:

The Sahara was at one time covered in water. In its sands lies the proof. Ancient plankton shells cover 24,000 square miles of it and can be seen from space satellites.

Temperature changes brought on by the movement of the oceans' water currents cause the winds to shift and move. As such, water vapor and great gusts blow, and the wind carries dust particles of the nutrient-rich phosphorous from the plankton. 7,000 tons of dust is airborn at any one time. The skyway it follows leads to South America and the Amazon.

The Amazon depends on this fertilizer, which becomes soluble as rains bring the rich fertilizer to the Amazon's otherwise nutrient-depleted soil. (It is short on phosphate.) It receives food and phosphates by rains from Saharan dust.

In turn, Amazonian trees and vegetation gives us about 20% of the Earth's oxygen. The Amazon has been called, "The Lungs of the

Earth." The rains fall 252 days of the year there. The fertility of this dust does not produce life until it is joined with water.

The waters of Antarctica also carry important life to our world. In the freezing and thawing of the water cycle, the freezing condenses the ice. As a result, small tubes form in the ice that expunge the portion that will not freeze that is rich in brine. This brine is heavier than the water itself and sinks two miles below the surface of the water.

It begins its journey of movement and flow within the currents and streams of the ocean floor. Upon settling into areas where underwater vents open to the Earth's crust, the brine heats up to 700 degrees Fahrenheit, at which temperature they melt rock.

The melting of this rock releases valuable minerals like sulfur and iron that help to feed life. The water currents where these minerals are present become soluble, and they flow near the surface where great plankton blooms occur.

Life explodes as the plankton feed and reproduce. Within twenty-four hours, plankton blooms can multiply, covering 500 square miles of ocean. This plankton serves as the base of the food chain for life in the sea.

Water is key to all life. It's time we go upstream.

CHAPTER FOUR
IN HIS PRESENCE

PRESSING IN

And he showed me a river of the water of life, clear as crystal, coming from the throne of God and of the Lamb, in the middle of its street. And on either side of the river was the tree of life, bearing twelve kinds of fruit, yielding its fruit every month; and the leaves of the tree were for the healing of the nations. (Revelation 22:1-2)

YHVH Himself is our source. The water of life, like a river, comes from the very throne of YHVH and of the Lamb: "There is a river whose streams make glad the city of God, the holy habitation of the Most High." (Psalm 46:4)

When we see that we are made mostly of water, when we notice that it makes life, we see our value in Him. We are made in His image, a part of Him and Heaven.

You are precious. Life is precious. Your life today at this time with the people you know is of great purpose.

Look into the starry night. Know how much man has searched for life. He has searched for water. He has searched for communication. It is here and it is in you.

Our water is precious. It is life. We are a part of it, and it is a part of us, and it is all part of the Creator.

In the Creator's efforts to do away with sin and bring about new life from the water, we find the example of Noah and the flood. The Earth was given a re-birth and new life out of water. This rebirth following a flood also closely matches some tribal creation stories from various cultures around the world.

> 9 This is the account of Noah and his family. Noah was a righteous man, blameless among the people of his time, and he walked faithfully with God. 10 Noah had three sons: Shem, Ham and Japheth. (Genesis 6:9-10)

YHVH chose Noah and his family to be saved and given a new, cleansed, and reborn earth. Noah was considered righteous and even blameless among people. He was faithful and walked with God. He was in the presence of God talking, listening and obeying. What a thing to be asked to do—to build a massive ark on dry ground.

As Pastor David Housholder once said, "Can you imagine Mrs. Noah saying to him, 'Why are you doing that?' and Noah saying, 'I just have to.'"

Noah's family helped, too. Then YHVH gave the command of continued intention of life and new life: He told Noah to place two of every kind of animal that has *breath*.

> "They went into the ark with Noah, two and two of all flesh in which there was the breath of life." (Genesis 15:7 ESV)

When Yahweh stopped the rains and the waters receded and

uncovered a new land, the dove had found a new place to land. The dove that so often represents the Spirit has found a new place to rest.

Before, amid the depravity of the creation, the Spirit of YHVH had no place to rest upon. Then the physical representation of the Spirit, again in the form of a dove, found a chute of life exemplified by a piece of olive leaf. It had found a living tree, a place to rest.

Mother Earth had come up from her own baptism.

The Creator didn't stop there. In researching olive trees, I found that their life span well outlast ours. They live for generations and even to 1,000 years old and still *bear fruit* with regular pruning and fertilizing. There is one olive tree growing in Western Crete that is believed to be 3,000-5,000 years old.

Not only did the dove find life to rest upon, but it found long, fruit-bearing life. Only God could create such imagery from the physical to the spiritual. If we're willing to look, we'll find that life and the Word are rich with this imagery.

Going a little further with the olive branch, we find more beautiful insights. How often are we pressed to the point where afterward, a beautiful strength and light and spiritual power and presence comes upon us after God has seen us through?

Olive oil is derived from pressing. Following the pressing, it takes time before that oil rises up from the waters of the fruit. Oil in Biblical times was used in consecrating, helping the skin, used with food, and as fuel for the light of their lamps.

The people that I know who have a strong walk in faith and have the brightest impact in my life have often been people who have undergone great difficulty and risen above by the grace of God.

"We are hard pressed on every side, but not crushed; perplexed, but not in despair." (2 Corinthians 4:8 NIV)

Their light shines, so to speak, fueled by the oil born from extreme faithfulness in all types of pressings.

∼

Yeshua/Jesus was most pressed the night before his crucifixion in the Garden of Gethsemane. "Gethsemane" means "olive press." He knew what was coming, and this pressing brought forth drops of blood instead of sweat as he prayed to the Father, asking Him three times to not have to go through with it. The weight of sin of humanity was beginning to be placed upon Him.

In 142 B.C., when the Hellenistic Greeks had overtaken the Temple, a Hebrew clan, the Maccabbes, regained the Temple and the sacred items from the tabernacle. According to the story associated with Hannukah, the Maccabbes found only one container of oil—enough to light the golden lamp stand for one day. Yet miraculously, the oil burned for eight days, the amount of time needed to make new oil.

The number eight in Hebrew historically carried the meaning for new beginnings, and it still does. An eight-piece menorah was constructed to represent the miracle of light and celebrated as Hanukkah. (Eight marks the first day of a new week. In music theory, a new octave begins again every eighth note.)

There is also a ninth branch made to the menorah and this piece is called the *Shamash*, which means "helper" or "servant light."(Breaking Matzo"The History and Meaning of the Menorah") We see a reference to His Spirit as such in the New Testament in John 14:26 (ESV): But the Helper, the Holy Spirit, whom the Father will send in my name, he will teach you all things and bring to your remembrance all that I have said to you.

Christ's death and resurrection, along with Noah and the flood, were spoken about together in 1 Peter 3:20-21:

20 because they formerly did not obey, when God's patience waited in the days of Noah, while the ark was being prepared, in which a few, that is, eight persons, were brought safely through water. 21 Baptism, which corresponds to this, now saves you, not as a removal of dirt from the body but as an appeal to God for a good conscience, through the resurrection of Jesus Christ...

YHVH saved eight people. His evident use of this for a "new beginning" as well as baptism corresponds with the flood.

After the flood, and after the waters receded, YHVH shows Himself in the waters in another way: by setting a rainbow in the sky as the symbol of His promise to Noah.

Each rainbow begins with millions of tiny water droplets. The rain droplets serve as a type of reflector of light. White light enters one individual rain droplet and exits as one specific color of the spectrum. Without millions of water droplets, a rainbow would not occur. (Faculty.cord.edu "How a Rainbow is Formed" by Gena Mahlen)

Take a moment and let this verse sink in:

Like the appearance of a rainbow in the clouds on a rainy day, so was the radiance around him. This was the appearance of the likeness of the glory of YHVH. When I saw it, I fell facedown, and I heard the voice of the one speaking. (Ezekiel 1:28)

The essence of water and light is all about Him.

In the spring and summer of 2014, scientists discovered that there are oceans' worth of water in the mantle of the Earth. Here is one of the links: http://www.natureworldnews.com/articles/5792/20140127/oceans-worth-water-trapped-beneath-earths-mantle.htm

Now consider this passage of scripture from Genesis 8:1-2:

> But God remembered Noah and all the beasts and all the cattle that were with him in the ark; and God caused a wind to pass over the earth, and the water subsided. 2 Also the fountains of the deep and the floodgates of the sky were closed, and the rain from the sky was restrained.

At the beginning of studying and reading this book, you saw the word about the child being born after the water broke, and the child was "delivered." YHVH shows this part of life many times in the Word, both in the physical and spiritual.

Reading about Moses and the Exodus from Egypt, the Hebrew slaves are pressed up against the Red Sea with no escape. The Egyptians are closing in.

Not until it looked absolutely hopeless did YHVH show His glory. He parted the waters and *delivered* the Hebrews into a new life of freedom from captivity.

Before delivering my children, I experienced the greatest pain in my life. Were it not for all of the other women that gave birth before me, I would have thought I would die. I think of the first woman, Eve, delivering the first baby and probably thinking she was going to die. But then instead, life bursts out.

Within the womb, the child was safe and snug and growing. But eventually the womb becomes a form of captivity, as it no longer offers the space to float and move freely about. Then the waters break, and a new life and freedom are gained as the child passes through; delivered.

In order to save Moses' life as an infant, his parents placed him in a basket and floated on the Nile. He was drawn out from the waters of the Nile and given a new life, to be raised by Pharaoh's daughter.

"When the child grew older, she brought him to Pharaoh's daughter, and he became her son. She named him Moses, 'Because,' she said, 'I drew him out of the water.'" (Exodus 2:10 ESV)

Exodus 13:21-14:29 is the message of YHVH's presence and deliverance of the people. They saw His presence physically in the cloud by day and the pillar of fire by night. The people had to learn to keep their eyes on them and follow and trust.

YHVH often uses paradox to reveal Himself: fire and water, the beginning and the end, the Lion of Judah and the Lamb that was slain. The cloud and the pillar of fire had been leading them, but Moses tells them they will not need to fight or even lift a finger, for God will fight for them.

We read that the Angel of the LORD moves behind them, as well as the pillar of cloud, to protect them from the back. The Egyptians couldn't see them because the cloud became darkness to them.

Early the next morning, the Creator/YHVH looked down from the pillar of fire and cloud and threw the Egyptians into confusion, so much so that the Egyptians recognized YHVH was fighting against them.

At this point, I was wondering how fire was also a part of God in the way of life. It isn't as frequently used in the Bible, but it *is* used, and it is more than just an antithesis to water. In the natural, science has also found and observed that fire promotes life. It is most notable in Northern Canada.

This information comes from *Earth From Space*, by NOVA PBS Video online.

As the great timbers die or become diseased, the ingredients for creating new life are locked inside: carbon, sulfur, and phosphorous. The normal process of releasing these elements happens quite slowly through rot and decay; it can take decades. However, fire can shorten the cycle to a matter of hours.

Oxygen fuels the flames, and the resins and saps within pine trees are highly flammable. Fire is rapid oxidation. The nutrients kept inside the trees are released in the ash, which becomes food and nutrition for a burst of new life following every blaze.

Years ago, I traveled through the Black Hills/Paha Sapa in South Dakota. I passed multiple charred tree trunks that managed to remain standing, but there were no branches or anything smaller than the trunks because the fire had consumed them.

However, I saw opened spaces covered in fresh new grasses and shoots of saplings in their tender chartreuse and green of youth. Life was springing up across the hillside.

We also see fire used symbolically with regard to the Holy Spirit in the book of Acts.

"They saw what seemed to be tongues of fire that separated and came to rest on each of them, All of them were filled with the Holy Spirit and began to speak in other tongues as the Spirit enabled them." (Acts 2:3-4)

This marked the beginning of new life in His Spirit and moving forward in living a life of teaching the Good News through His Spirit's power. It happened swiftly—decades'-worth of spiritual maturity came in an instant.

They were changed, and everything that was spiritually dead or diseased no longer mattered because they had become alive in power and life through His Spirit. We will return to this scripture again.

Several years ago, my young son was changing schools because of boundary changes in our city, and I was concerned for him. I had prayed he would find new friends, that he would have a teacher that worked well with little boys, and that YHVH would bless him. At the end of summer break before school started, we had that special visit to his new school.

We met his wonderful teacher, and she showed us where he would be seated in their classroom. To our surprise, next to his name on the table was the name of his best friend from the old school.

I was so excited. The teacher marveled as she explained she had no idea that they were friends. She then put up a slide show presentation about herself as an introduction to who she was. She had photos of her family, and she had two young sons. She knew all about little boys.

As I left through the school doors and walked down the sunny sidewalk, quietly smiling to myself, I distinctly heard YHVH speak in a joking way, "Do you see Me now?"

I laughed out loud and replied, "Yes!"

When I have my own doubts and worries and fears, I come to the place where YHVH makes it all work out. He still sometimes says to me jokingly after He makes good, "Do you see Me now?" His presence was always there—it just took a while before I recognized it.

He showed Himself very boldly to the Israelites, and still they forgot or complained or became complacent with His presence and disobeyed. But every day they were provided manna, a sustaining bread from Heaven and the miracle of God's very obvious presence:

When the dew fell upon the camp in the night, the manna fell with it. (Numbers 11:9 ESV)

The manna fell with the dew—the waters. God's presence and Spirit are again associated with water/dew and with the bread. The fullness of Trinity is exemplified spiritually by the physical manifestations.

The wandering lasted for forty years until those who had not fulfilled God's will of faith and obedience had passed on. Those people would not go into the Promised Land. Joshua and the ones who were of the next generation were able to go into the Promised Land.

YHVH led this group through water, too, before reaching their new life.

In Joshua 3:1-14, the Creator opened the Jordan River for them to cross to reach a whole new life. His use of water and new birth vibrantly points to life and God as the Giver of life.

Take a moment and read that passage. If you don't have a Bible, you can look it up on your smartphone. Let this revelation reach you as He shows you His ways. He is involved in depths He wants us to recognize now.

Nothing is off limits for YHVH in the Bible, and it is especially so with sexuality. Sex is the means and place where the conception of life occurs. Leviticus 15 is all about purity and being clean in relationship to sexuality and, ultimately, life. YHVH is showing how important life is in its earliest forms.

In the Levitical Law, if death comes to the egg or when the woman's moon or menstruation happens, a woman is considered unclean. A man's emission/ejaculation, if not within his wife, is considered an impurity under the Levitical Law. His seed is dead and not used for life.

Great lengths had to be taken to bring one back into cleanliness. It included the washing of items, bathing of the person, and rinsing clean. Even the things he or she touches or sits on are considered unclean unless they are washed. Both the women and the men had to individually bathe.

Even following the menstrual flow and ritual cleansing, women were not allowed to have sex for a time afterward, either. The timing when they were permitted to have sex again coincided with a time of fertility and ovulation.

Again, the implication is for life. It was a cleansing from what was not life to what may become life. This was a big part of their lifestyle, and it is still used to varying degrees by practicing Jews.

Bathing for ritual cleansing took place in what is called a *mikveh*. The use of a *mikveh* is a Hebrew term for a place of fresh water for cleansing and purity purposes. It needed to be filled with spring water, moving water, or fresh rainwater.

Mikvehs were sometimes found in caves surrounded by rocks or dug deep into the ground until they reached the spring that would then bubble up. There are still ancient *mikvehs* in Israel.

In synagogues today, *mikvehs* are often built into part of the building. They resemble a sort of spa bath. Jewish couples still often use them independent of each other before marriage. It is the symbolic cleansing of the old life and into the new life of marriage, which ultimately can create a life. (My Jewish Learning.com "What is a Mikveh?" by Shoshanna Lockshin)

When you see a *mikveh* or envision the use of one, it is easy to associate it with the act of baptism. Some of the ancient *mikvehs* even look womb-like—a place of new life and rebirth.

"I baptize you with water for repentance. But after me comes one who is more powerful than I, whose sandals I am not worthy to carry. He will baptize you with the Holy Spirit and fire." (Matthew 3:11)

It is the old spiritual life ending and the beginning of going into a new spiritual life.

> "Then Jesus came from Galilee to the Jordan to be baptized by John. But John tried to deter him, saying, 'I need to be baptized by you, and do you come to me?'
>
> Jesus replied, 'Let it be so now; it is proper for us to do this to fulfill all righteousness.' Then John consented. As soon as Jesus was baptized, he went up out of the water..." (Matthew 3:13-15 NIV)

Here we read that John didn't feel worthy enough, yet he desired to be obedient. We see Jesus, who is completely free of sin, still desiring to be baptized, symbolizing what God desires and attributing it to righteousness. It is obedience.

You can imagine the impact if people were free to say, "Well, Jesus didn't get baptized." Yet even Jesus did it, and he said it would fulfill all righteousness.

It was a birth for Him, and from this place of coming up from the waters of the River Jordan into a new time of His life, His public ministry began. He remains blameless. He did not have impurities to cleanse, but He was living by example.

Life is difficult for all of us. The war that begins after baptism is even harder. By getting baptized, you have proclaimed war against an enemy: the evil spirit, Satan himself.

After the baptism, Yeshua was led to the wilderness to be tempted by Satan. Yet through that, Yeshua showed that the Enemy can be defeated with the powerful Word of Yahweh.

Every year, the Jewish festival called Sukkot is celebrated. It is an eight-day festival of remembering the Israelites and the forty years of traveling with tents as temporary dwelling places.

Hebrews would come with their own booths or tents and live in mass community as they celebrated together. This festival also included praying for rains and waters to come.

Yeshua/Jesus attended this festival. This is what happened in John 7:37-38: "On the last and greatest day of the festival, Jesus stood and said in a loud voice, 'Let anyone who is thirsty come to me and drink. 38 Whoever believes in me, as Scripture has said, rivers of living water will flow from within them.'"

It reads that it happened on the last and greatest day of the festival, complete with a big water celebration as the chief priests poured pitcher after pitcher of water to the cheers and celebration of the people.

This was the eighth day. As we discussed earlier, eight in Hebrew has the symbolism of a "new beginning." This was the day that Yeshua/Jesus announced Himself as the source of life and living.

Rains are necessary for life, for bearing fruit and a harvest. The waters are also the Spirit of Christ producing life and a *fullness* of life that is productive and fruitful through His Spirit.

When you see how Yeshua/Jesus states this in the spiritual with the physical, you see a powerful way of who you are in body and spirit through Him. You are purposely and preciously made for the amazing life of relationship that He provides.

~

Going back to Leviticus, we see how God placed so many things in the physical elements that symbolize the spiritual. Leviticus is fascinating this way; many people grow bored with reading it, but when you begin to ask Yahweh/YHVH to show you His meanings in these things, it becomes a thrilling book.

> Then the priest shall order that one of the birds be killed over fresh water in a clay pot. 6 He is then to take the live bird and dip it, together with the cedar wood, the scarlet yarn and the hyssop, into the blood of the bird that was killed over the fresh water. 7 Seven times he shall sprinkle the one to be cleansed of the defiling disease, and then pronounce them clean. After that, he is to release the live bird in the open fields. (Leviticus 14:5-7)

This procedure was for the cleansing of a skin disease—a "flesh" disease. There is symbolism in that. Our human condition and sinful nature is often referred to as *flesh* in the Word.

Skin is mostly made up of water. When it is dry, it flakes. Much of our household dust comes from our skin. (*Analytical Chemistry* "Tracing the Chemistry of Household Dust" by Janet Pelley Feb. 7, 2017) This puts a spin on the saying, "ashes to ashes, dust to dust" when someone has died. Our skin contains the earthly part of dust.

Even raindrops, which are water, return to Earth because of the dust particles in the drop of water. That dust returns the water back to Earth.

Upon going through the ritual of the cleansing of skin, they use two birds (doves). The first one is killed over a clay jar filled with fresh water. Interestingly, the Word of God calls *us* clay jars:

> "But we have this treasure in jars of clay to show that this all-surpassing power is from God and not from us." (2 Corinthians 4:7)

See the symbolism? The fresh water is within the clay jar in the Levitical cleansing of skin disease and in this verse in 2 Corinthians, the surpassing power within the clay jars comes from Yahweh. In keeping with what we are being led to see, the fresh water is the reminder of what is of Yahweh.

Continuing with the Levitical steps, the person is then to take the live bird and dip it into the blood of the sacrificed bird along with cedar wood, scarlet thread, and hyssop. The cedar wood and hyssop represent internal and external spiritual and physical truths.

One of the woods believed to be part of the cross Yeshua/Jesus was crucified on was made of cedar. (HistoryandHeadlines.com "March 21, 630: The True Cross is Returned to Jerusalem")Scripture does state that the sponge soaked in vinegar that was lifted to Yeshua/Jesus' mouth was on a hyssop branch. This happened while He hung on the cross, pierced to this tree, when He said, "I thirst."

> "A jar full of sour wine stood there, so they put a sponge full of the sour wine on a hyssop branch and held it to his mouth. (John 19:29 ESV)"

The scarlet thread in color represents both sin and the color of the blood that is needed to make the payment for the sin. After the person is pronounced cleansed, the live bird is released into an open field, which represents our inheritance.

This is freedom in Christ, meaning the anointed One, Yeshua/Jesus, that we are given and the resurrection of new life through His sacrifice.

The dove/pigeon is symbolic of the Holy Spirit. It is by the power of the Holy Spirit that Jesus was resurrected. In the earthly tradition of performing this act, a bird did not literally die and come back to life.

It was only through the Anointed One, the Christ, by His Holy Spirit, that anyone came back to life. So the two different birds were used to symbolize both the sacrificial death and the life and freedom that comes with the remission of sin.

> But when Christ came as high priest of the good things that are now already here, he went through the greater and more perfect tabernacle that is not made with human hands, that is to say, is not a part of this creation. 12 He did not enter by means of the blood of goats and calves; but he entered the Most Holy Place once for all by his own blood, thus obtaining eternal redemption. 13 The blood of goats and bulls and the ashes of a heifer sprinkled on those who are ceremonially unclean sanctify them so that they are outwardly clean. 14 How much more, then, will the blood of Christ, who through the eternal Spirit offered himself unblemished to God, cleanse our consciences from acts that lead to death, so that we may serve the living God! 15 For this reason Christ is the mediator of a new covenant, that those who are called may receive the promised eternal inheritance—now that he has died as a ransom to set them free from the sins committed under the first covenant... (Hebrews 9:11-15)

You know I want to say it... "Do you see Me now?"

The clay jar (us), filled with fresh water (the Spirit of Jesus, our Living Water), comes from within our spirit through Him and His Spirit. We are cleansed in new life and the New Covenant of not just outward cleansing, but internal. Thus, we receive eternal freedom and life.

This scripture from John 19:34 used to bewilder me, but now it confirms all of these things. As Yeshua/Jesus hung on the cross and had died, the verse reads, "One of the soldiers, however, pierced his side with a spear, and immediately blood and water flowed out."

Blood is the *identity* of our earthly life.

The importance of the blood sacrifice meant there was a death as payment for sin. Sin equaled death and had no place with life with God. Even the blood that was shed had to come from animals that were considered without blemish.

This sacrifice was only good for one year. In order for blood to be given as a sacrifice, Yahweh/YHVH had to become man to be blood perfected enough to serve as a sacrifice once and for all.

There is no purer blood than the blood of Christ, which He gave out of the purest love of all time.

I have gone from having much to having little, losing family, positions, and more. The pain of that is difficult. I cannot imagine the love of Christ, to give up all the glory of Heaven, the throne, and perfection. Then He became like a man born in the lowliest of places, to be present with us and to be the blood sacrifice for all His creation and our sin.

Not only was he lowly but he also suffered a painful death. Worse than that, he had known no sin and no separation from His pure holiness away from the Father.

Often, our greatest fears are in the unknown. The anguish Yeshua felt at Gethsemane was evidenced in sweating drops of blood. For the first time in a sinless body, he was going to experience the sensation of sin pressed upon Him. But it wasn't just one person's sin; it was the world's sin and its curse.

He gives us physical ways to see Him and know Him. This is how we know that He loves us. "But God demonstrates his own love for us in this: While we were still sinners, Christ died for us." (Romans 5:8)

This was for the sins of our flesh, our human imperfection, just like the unclean or diseased flesh found in the cleansing steps in Leviticus.

"For the life of the flesh is in the blood, and I have given it for you on the altar to make atonement for your souls, for it is the blood that makes atonement by the life." (Leviticus 17:11 ESV)

Yeshua had to become flesh to make the blood to sacrifice for us.

Leviticus 17:13 also points to the earthly nature of blood: "Any one also of the people of Israel, or of the strangers who sojourn among them, who takes in hunting any beast or bird that may be eaten shall pour out its blood and cover it with earth."

Blood carried the life on earth and also the sin. The blood was not to be eaten; it was to be returned to the Earth and covered.

Blood also had a voice, as the Bible speaks of the blood of Abel crying out from the ground as well as the blood of martyrs.

When Yeshua offers the cup of wine at the Last Supper with the disciples, he has them drink and says that it is his blood of the covenant (promise) poured out for many. This rocked the was Jewish law and tradition of the day.

But because of the purity of his blood (and his alone), it was the only one that could be represented spiritually to metaphorically "drink" in its spiritual purity. It is a remembrance of his presence with us and fulfilling the promise and new covenant with us as our sacrifice and His life for ours.

That night, He was taken into custody, and the next day he was crucified for us. His blood became a new wine.

His pursuit to bring us into a perfected relationship with Him comes out of incredible love and with the intention of a redeemed Creation.

It was not so He would win our affections but so we would know His great affection for us.

It is His heart for His beloved Creation and the freedom to love Him, if we choose.

CHAPTER FIVE
APPEARING

TANGIBLE PRESENCE

References to water in the Scriptures are frequent and continually associated with life and the Giver of Life. His powerful presence keeps popping up like clouds. His direct association with the clouds starts early on in the Word. Clouds are made up of tiny drops of *water*.

> When Moses went up on the mountain, the cloud covered it, 16 and the glory of the LORD settled on Mount Sinai. For six days the cloud covered the mountain, and on the seventh day the LORD called to Moses from within the cloud. 17 To the Israelites the glory of the LORD looked like a consuming fire on top of the mountain. 18 Then Moses entered the cloud as he went on up the mountain. And he stayed on the mountain forty days and forty nights. (Exodus 24:15-18)

YHVH continued to show His presence in the cloud and the fire in Numbers 9:15: "On the day the Tabernacle was set up, the cloud covered it. But from evening until morning the cloud over the Tabernacle looked like a pillar of fire."

And then He showed it again in Exodus 40:34-37:

> Then the cloud covered the Tent of Meeting, and the glory of the Lord filled the tabernacle. 35 Moses could not enter the Tent of Meeting because the cloud had settled upon it, and the glory of the Lord filled the tabernacle. 36 In all the travels of the Israelites, whenever the cloud lifted from above the tabernacle, they would set out; 37 but if the cloud did not lift, they did not set out—until the day it lifted. 38 So the cloud of the Lord was over the tabernacle by day, and fire was in the cloud by night, in the sight of all the house of Israel during all their travels.

We know that both water and fire bring about new life and God revealed His presence in both.

I have a girlfriend who suffered a great heartbreak. Her husband left her. She lost her home and her job. Her children were grown, and she felt as if she had nothing to live for except loneliness and pain. She couldn't bear it and told YHVH she didn't want to live anymore and didn't think she would.

She was returning from a trip visiting one of her children in another state, and as she flew in the airplane, her return to emptiness and loss was more than she could bear. She finished telling YHVH her plans for ending her life, then she opened the shade of the airplane window.

This is what she saw.

A pillar of fire amid the clouds. She took several photos and her life was never the same again. She knew she wasn't alone. (Photo used by permission)

In that moment, she knew who was with her on her travels through life. She would live. She dwelled in His presence in prayer, and He revealed His presence to her in a miraculous way.

This is the power of YHVH active today. He didn't just do this stuff in Biblical times. He continues to interact with us and through us to bring us new life. Even in the loss, she has experienced a much greater gain: new life and continued beauty that rises up from the ashes.

Let's return to Acts chapter 2.

---

1 When the day of Pentecost came, they were all together in one place. 2 Suddenly a sound like the blowing of a violent wind came from heaven and filled the whole house where they were sitting. 3 They saw what seemed to be tongues of fire that separated and came to rest on each of them. 4 All of them were filled with the Holy Spirit and began to speak in other tongues as the Spirit enabled them. (Acts 2:1-4)

His Holy Spirit came and began to dwell in and on man. Note the words "a violent wind from Heaven." Remember that *Ruah* also means "wind."

This happened after Yeshua resurrected and returned to Heaven. He had directed those who believed in Him as the Christ to wait for the coming of the power of the Holy Spirit. Sin was defeated by the perfect blood and sacrifice of Yeshua, and man was made clean and no longer separated from the presence of His Spirit. The Spirit arrived with great power.

The Hebrew word *Shekina* is a derivative of *mishkan*, which is a dwelling place, and *shakan*, which means presence. *Shekina* is used throughout Isaiah as a feminine form of a word meaning God's presence and dwelling place. (Wikipedia .org Shekinah)

When I remember my vision of the dove of breath, which was His Spirit, I remember the beautiful grace, elegance and flow to it—as lovely as anything I had ever seen. The word *Shekina*, a feminine form of a word to link His presence, made sense to me. There was that kind of femininity to the vision that was like a dove.

Genesis 1:27 reads, "So God created mankind in his own image, in the image of God he created them; male and female he created them."

As He poured His spirit upon me while I was studying this, so much became clear. Review again this passage from 1 John 5, after having learned all that you have, see how much more clearly He is revealing things to you.

6This is He who came by water and blood—Jesus Christ; not only by water, but by water and blood. And it is the Spirit who bears witness, because the Spirit is truth. 7For there are three that bear witness [b]in heaven: the Father, the Word, and the Holy Spirit; and these three are one. 8And there are three that bear witness on earth: the Spirit, the water, and the blood; and these three agree as one.

> 9If we receive the witness of men, the witness of God is greater; for this is the witness of [c]God which He has testified of His Son. 10He who believes in the Son of God has the witness in himself; he who does not believe God has made Him a liar, because he has not believed the testimony that God has given of His Son. 11And this is the testimony: that God has given us eternal life, and this life is in His Son. 12He who has the Son has [d]life; he who does not have the Son of God does not have life. 13These things I have written to you who believe in the name of the Son of God, that you may know that you have eternal life, [e]and that you may *continue to* believe in the name of the Son of God.(1 John 5:6-13 NKJV)

And we have received it in Yeshua's own words. Please read this part carefully and really think about them in light of what has recently been revealed. I am using the Aramaic translation which was a common language spoken in Yeshua's time. This translation in these verses is powerful.

> Yeshua answered and said to him: "Timeless truth I am telling you: 'If a person is not born from water and The Spirit, it is impossible that he shall enter the Kingdom of God. 6That which is born from flesh is flesh, and that which is born from The Spirit is spirit. 7Do not be surprised that I said to you that all of you must be born again. 8The Spirit breathes where he will, and you hear his voice, but you do not know from where he comes and where he goes; thus is everyone who is born from The Spirit.'" (John 3:5-8 Aramaic Bible in Plain English)

His revelation of Himself in association with these waters is grace itself. His Spirit is grace, His life that He gives us is by His grace, His forgiveness is His grace, and His incredible steadfast presence in and throughout our life is flooded by His grace and love.

There is something marvelous in the water. It is the essence of a profound part of our life, creation, and His presence, and it brings to us the fullness of life as we live in the way we were created: in the image of God. What comes next from this foundation is the understanding of the power and spirituality of our words, prayers, blessings, and praise.

I pray that you are being moved in new ways as your eyes, heart, and mind receive from Him. YHVH loves you and desires your time, your attention, your friendship, and your plans. He wants you to know He is there any time and anywhere. He is interested in all parts of your life. He desires you to have hope in Him. He wants you to know how much you are loved.

He desires you to know Him more deeply in all areas of life here both *physically* and *spiritually*, for He is in it all. Belong to Him, and He belongs to you. Heaven rejoices in a child coming home.

We have received so much from His Word to give praise and thanks for. Continue in your times of praise and thoughts on Him. Pay attention to the constant rhythm of your breath. It moves as you move. It is not stagnant, and it is ever-present. So is the work of His Spirit in your life.

I have found that when I go to bed and I turn over to fall asleep, I think of YHVH and praise Him, and I sleep well. I wake in the morning thinking of Him and praise Him again.

After a while, the bed and sleep turns into a sanctuary of peace. If I do wake in the night, I use the time to pray for others or praise Him more. It has changed the feeling of my bedroom. There is a peace in there that feels like the peace I find when I walk into a sanctuary. It is a sanctuary. There is a joy in the time of rest.

This is a list of some Bible verses about coming into the presence of YHVH. You could pause and write them down or come back to them, but I suggest you read them all and apply their truth to your life.

- Psalm 16:11

- Psalm 42:1
- Psalm 43:3
- Psalm 145:18
- Isaiah 55:3
- Isaiah 55:6
- Matthew 6:6
- John 4:6
- Romans 5:1-2
- Hebrews 4:16
- Hebrews 7:19
- Hebrews 10:19-23
- Hebrews 11:6
- James 4:8
- Ephesians 2:13
- Ephesians 3:12
- 1 Peter 3:18

YHVH/Yahweh continually promised through the Old Testament and spoke in many ways of Yeshua. We receive assurance that He fulfills His promises and that His Words are confirmed in truth all the way through Scripture.

As the scarlet thread runs through His Word, we are pursued by an ever-present Creator showing Himself with arms opened wide saying, "Here I Am, come to Me. Receive." He wants to free us so that when life's hard times come, they will not overcome us.

We can find rest and sleep like when Yeshua slept on the boat during a storm while those with less faith feared for their lives. Grace upon grace. Yeshua spoke to the wind and waves, "Peace, be still." Those words are also meant for us.

I will sprinkle clean water on you, and you will be clean; I will cleanse you from all your impurities and from all your idols. 26 I will give you a new heart and put a new spirit in you; I will remove from you your heart of stone and give you a heart of flesh. (Ezekiel 36:25-26)

Paradox Presence

- The Lamb that was slain and the Lion of Judah
- We die so that we may live, also seen in the death and resurrection
- He is the first and the last, the Alpha and Omega
- He is a servant and the King of Kings

It is no surprise to see the Lord manifest His presence in both water and fire.

From the tongues of fire in Acts, He also spoke to Moses from a burning bush that was not consumed.

The scripture of Isaiah 43:2 reads, "When you pass through the waters, I will be with you; and when you pass through the rivers, they will not sweep over you. When you walk through the fire, you will not be burned; the flames will not set you ablaze."

Yahweh/YHVH proved those points in the physical through the Old Testament as He led them through the waters into a new life. He also kept the men in the book of Daniel, who were thrown into the fiery furnace, alive. They didn't even smell like smoke afterward.

Now we see the evidence of His Spirit in the ways of water and fire and in Christ: it is His presence of His Spirit in and upon us.

Yahweh/YHVH evidenced His presence as well as guided them by it. We are given His Spirit. The breath of Yeshua blown upon us where we now are able to walk and be led by His Spirit.

As we come more frequently into the presence of YHVH in praise, prayer, and worship, we recognize how to sense Him. We become more familiar with His moving in our lives. We begin to recognize how to keep in step with Him and be led to a higher and deeper intimacy with greater purpose for our lives.

YHVH showed Himself in the physical and continues to do so at different times. His greatest manifestation of Himself in the physical was Christ.

> "Jesus replied, 'Have I been with you all this time, Philip, and yet you still don't know who I am? Anyone who has seen me has seen the Father! So why are you asking me to show him to you?'" (John 14:9 NLT)

As Christ walked the Earth, the essence of YHVH and Heaven also manifested in the clouds. Read these scriptures and notice the association in them remembering they are made up of water.

> In my vision at night I looked, and there before me was one like a son of man, coming with the clouds of heaven. He approached the Ancient of Days and was led into his presence. (Daniel 7:13)

> And I heard a man's voice between the banks of the Ulai, and it called, "Gabriel, make this man understand the vision." (Daniel 8:16)

(The Ulai is the name of the river or canal, and Daniel was hearing a voice come from it, which was in command over the angel Gabriel. His voice came from the place of the water. Gabriel is also the angel sent to Mary to give her the message that she would give birth to the Messiah.)

Yeshua said, "I Am. And you will see the Son of Man seated in the place of power at Yahweh's right hand and coming on the clouds of heaven." (Mark 14:62)

---

¹Now after six days Jesus took Peter, James, and John his brother, led them up on a high mountain by themselves; 2and He was transfigured before them. His face shone like the sun, and His clothes became as white as the light. 3And behold, Moses and Elijah appeared to them, talking with Him. 4Then Peter answered and said to Jesus, "Lord, it is good for us to be here; if You wish, [a]let us make here three tabernacles: one for You, one for Moses, and one for Elijah."

5While he was still speaking, behold, a bright cloud overshadowed them; and suddenly a voice came out of the cloud, saying, "This is My beloved Son, in whom I am well pleased. Hear Him!" 6And when the disciples heard *it,* they fell on their faces and were greatly afraid. 7But Jesus came and touched them and said, "Arise, and do not be afraid." 8When they had lifted up their eyes, they saw no one but Jesus only. (Matthew 17:1-8 NKJ)

The former account I made, O Theophilus, of all that Jesus began both to do and teach, 2until the day in which [a]He was taken up, after He through the Holy Spirit had given commandments to the apostles whom He had chosen, 3to whom He also presented Himself alive after His suffering by many [b]infallible proofs, being seen by them during forty days and speaking of the things pertaining to the kingdom of God.

4And being assembled together with *them,* He commanded them not to depart from Jerusalem, but to wait for the Promise of the Father, "which," *He said,* "you have heard from Me; 5for John truly baptized with water, but you shall be baptized with the Holy Spirit not many days from now." 6Therefore, when they had come together, they asked Him, saying, "Lord, will You at this time restore the kingdom to Israel?" 7And He said to them, "It is not for you to know times or seasons which the Father has put in His own authority. 8But you shall receive power when the Holy Spirit has come upon you; and you shall be [c]witnesses to Me in Jerusalem, and in all Judea and Samaria, and to the end of the earth."

9Now when He had spoken these things, while they watched, He was taken up, and *a cloud received* Him out of their sight. 10And while they looked steadfastly toward heaven as He went up, behold, two men stood by them in white apparel, 11who also said, "Men of Galilee, why do you stand gazing up into heaven? This *same* Jesus, who was taken up from you into heaven, will so come in like manner as you saw Him go into heaven." (Acts 1:1-11 NKJ)

Look, he is coming with the *clouds,* and every eye will see him, even those who pierced him; and all the peoples of the earth will mourn because of him. So shall it be! Amen. (Revelation 1:7)

YHVH's presence and new life is consistently revealed in association with forms of water, of which we are mostly made.

YHVH/the Creator also points clearly to where water is *not* present and what He desires to free us from: "As for you, because of the blood of my covenant with you, I will free your prisoners from the waterless pit." (Zechariah 9:11)

You have been growing in the understanding of how you are made and the ways and presence of YHVH's Spirit. Prayer and intimacy with Him is the heart of our relationship. He seeks our presence and desires to give us the gifts of His Kingdom and Spirit.

As I am writing this portion of the book, fires are burning in Colorado Springs, CO, and rains have flooded parts of northern Florida. I see the devastation to the property and belongings of people as they are evacuating and fleeing the area. I don't understand the purpose behind these disasters, but the exact timing of these two elements has my attention.

A reporter interviewed a woman whose home succumbed to the fire in Colorado Springs. She was dirty, hot, and sweating, and her hair was mussed. Her cross necklace stuck to her sweat-soaked skin. As she spoke, she wept and pulled from herself an inner faith so strong. "Yes, this is happening," she said, "but God is good. Something good will come from this."

She knew her Lord, and she trusted Him, and He is delivering her through the flame without her faith and spirit perishing. She anticipates new life.

When we walk with Him, hard times don't consume us. His presence is His Spirit, the grace and strength that keeps us moving forward in hope. These are the treasures from Heaven that are not consumed, and there will be new life.

Through tears that sometimes fall, the incredible presence of God's life-giving waters within us roll down our cheeks. A reminder of His nearness is in the essence of those tears and in Psalm 134:18: "The Lord is near to the brokenhearted and saves the crushed in spirit."

And also in Psalm 56:8: "You have kept count of my tossings; put my tears in your bottle. Are they not in your book?"

Then, when we are finally face to face, it promises in Revelation 21:3-5:

---

3 And I heard a loud voice from the throne, saying, "Behold, the tabernacle of YHVH is among men, and He will dwell among

them, and they shall be His people, and YHVH Himself will be among them, 4 and He will wipe away every tear from their eyes; and there will no longer be any death; there will no longer be any mourning, or crying, or pain; the first things have passed away." 5 And He who sits on the throne said, "Behold, I am making all things new." And He said, "Write, for these words are faithful and true."

In all these physical examples of water, there is a sacredness. Realizing this kind of sacredness reveals the presence of YHVH. The foundation is set to begin to comprehend the power of words born from sacred breath.

CHAPTER SIX
THE CREATOR SPEAKS

THE LIVING WORD

And YHVH said, "Let there be..."

"By the Word of YHVH were the heavens made and all their host by the breath of his mouth." (Psalm 33:6 AMP)

When we recognize the source of our gift and Who is the Living Word, we see the love we were created with. We see the Word's power when we look at Scripture. His breath is everywhere in it. We know it from living our lives and the power of words in our lives.

    We are intentionally and lovingly made for relationship. He loves you. He has poured Himself into you and He desires that you know Him and the life He intended for you. Through you, His love reaches others....

    ...a word.
    ...life.
    ...for you.
    ...for others.

He came so that you may have life and have it abundantly. He's about life, and His Word speaks it. Let's learn to live—really *live*—and move by His breath.

Learning that our words come on our exhaled breath, we also know the one major component that is different in our exhaled breath is water. Our words are *delivered* from our breath. This is the power and intensity they are *born* from. YHVH spoke creation into place.

The first words spoken to Adam were from YHVH. It was YHVH's language, and man understood it. This is why I find ancient languages and Hebrew so powerful in terms, spellings, and letters to a people that He called His.

YHVH's first words of communication were on relationships with His direction for their position and purpose as well as His provision for them. In relationship, He said that Eve was a *help* to Adam and that they were to multiply. It was a call for more life.

He told them their position by telling them to subdue the Earth and to be masters and have dominion. He also told them about His provision for them by all of the food He has given them to eat, as well as the provision of Eve's help.

Many have misinterpreted what a "master" is and what "dominion" is. It isn't a conquering; it isn't oppression. It is *protecting* and *caring* instead. The master takes charge of what has been given that is susceptible now to the one who has received it.

To honor the gift is to honor the role of caring for that gift. All of Creation lives in relationship to the Creator as we do. All Creation, it says, cries out for the sons of YHVH.

YHVH told Adam to name every kind of animal. Naming brings them into a relationship. YHVH desired a relationship between the animals and man. It is the power of words. It is an identity in a name that is honor.

In the same way, Yeshua gave position, provision and relationship instruction by his words in John 20:21-23:

Instruction and Position

21 Again Yeshua said, "Peace be with you! As the Father has sent me, I am sending you."

Provision

22 And with that he breathed on them and said, "Receive the Holy Spirit.

Relationship

23 If you forgive anyone's sins, their sins are forgiven; if you do not forgive them, they are not forgiven."

In this verse we see all three. We see position, provision, and relationship: "You did not choose me, but I chose you and appointed you that you should go and bear fruit and that your fruit should abide, so that whatever you ask the Father in my name, he may give it to you." (John 15:16 ESV)

We can see YHVH's direction through His words for their lives by His view of their high position, His provision, and the importance of relationships. There is no relationship in unforgiveness, but there is in forgiveness.

Relationships are the foundation of life.

They create life, and a life lived alone, without coming into contact with another, is typically unproductive. Everyone you meet or come into contact with has the potential to grow or improve another's life or your own.

Even in a negative exchange, you are able to take something from it and grow from it, if you allow for that. Positive words and actions in relationship are productive, growth-inspiring, and life-giving.

∼

Sometimes the relationships you come into can surprise you years later, even after you have lost contact with that individual. We had a wonderful example of that in a Bible study class I was teaching. Three women from the African country of Sudan were in my class. One of them shared her story.

She had escaped persecution with her husband and children years earlier and had come to America. Our church took them in and provided a place to live.

One day, she was out for a walk, pushing her new baby in a stroller. She recognized a man outside in the middle of moving into a home around the corner from hers. She had been a classmate of his when she was a little girl in Sudan.

He recognized her, too. It was an amazing connection, and their renewed friendship began to grow.

Seated next to her in our Bible class was the wife of that school friend. She, too, came from Sudan. They were now friends and attending a Bible study together along with sharing all that life has come to be in leaving their home country and starting a new life in America. And next to her classmate's wife sat the wife's sister-in-law, also from Sudan.

These three women, all in varying ways of coming into relationship with one another, were growing together in their relationship with YHVH. They were also in their own unique and special community that YHVH miraculously brought together. He provided for them so that during times of struggles of acclimating to a new culture, they had one another to understand where they had come from while raising children together in a new land. They were given strength together to be able to continue to celebrate and pass the culture they had come from collectively to their children.

They weren't alone. YHVH's hand and provision in their lives was powerful to recognize.

∽

In the beginning, the Creator/YHVH spoke to man. He started the relationship. He gave man the ability to speak back to Him. Communication in these great depths and degree became the essence of relationship with Him.

This is a definition of communication by the National Joint Committee for the Communicative Needs of Persons with Severe Disabilities:

"Any act by which one person gives to or receives from another person information about that person's needs, desires, perceptions, knowledge, or affective states. Communication may be intentional or unintentional, may involve conventional or unconventional signals, may take linguistic or nonlinguistic forms, and may occur through spoken or other modes." (1992, p. 2.)

It also creates *community*. When we stop talking to one another, or more so, *listening* to one another, there is a break down in relationship and community.

Our ability to communicate at such high levels is uniquely human. We have our spoken words and numerous other means of communicating like signs, written words, and Braille. A flag or banner can be waved and represent communication. We even have the ability to understand body language.

Communication is where relationships take place. Communication is a form of the word "commune." The definition of "commune" is to share one's intimate thoughts or feelings with someone (or something), especially when the exchange is on a spiritual level.

---

commune₁ *vb* [kə'mjuːn] 1. to talk or converse intimately 2. to experience strong emotion or spiritual feelings. (*Merriam Dictionary*)

The *King James Version Bible Dictionary* goes further by defining "commune" as, "to have intercourse in contemplation or meditation."

This is what God started with His breath. He, being the Word, brings the exchange of intimacy and relationship to commune with Him through our words and thoughts. Our thoughts are formed in words.

Still, I found myself working through this and being concerned about infants that have no words but have life and breath. How does God see this? As He has done multiple times in this study, He showed me a verse and then a confirming verse said by Yeshua:

"From the lips of children and infants you have ordained praise because of your enemies, to silence the foe and the avenger." (Psalm 8:2)

But when the chief priests and the teachers of the law saw the wonderful things he did and the children shouting in the temple area, "Hosanna to the Son of David," they were indignant. 16 "Do you hear what these children are saying?" they asked him. "Yes," replied Yeshua, "have you never read, 'From the lips of children and infants you have ordained praise?'" (Matthew 21:15-21)

Purpose and praises from the lips of children and infants!

Following this exchange, the Scripture shows Yeshua leaving them and going to Bethany. He spends the night and gets up in the morning and is hungry. He finds the fig tree that has not bore any fruit.

Yeshua curses the tree, which dries up and withers. The water from the tree is gone. Yeshua's curse brings death to the tree, and the tree was unworthy to live because it didn't produce any fruit.

This made me think again of the verse that reads, "from our lips are the fruit of the tree of life." As we have seen so much more depth in the meanings of events in the Bible, this event means more than just a tree not bearing fruit. It contains a deeper meaning.

Sometimes I think of these layers of God's Word like those of a rosebud. I can look at it, and if I didn't know better, I might think that's all there is. But if I give it time and my attention, I know that as it opens, there are many petals and even a fragrance. Yahweh's Word is so much like that.

It goes on in this passage in Matthew 21:20-22

> When the disciples saw this, they were amazed. "How did the fig tree wither so quickly?" they asked. 21 Jesus replied, "I tell you the truth, if you have faith and do not doubt, not only can you do what was done to the fig tree, but also you can say to this mountain, 'Go, throw yourself into the sea,' and it will be done. 22 If you believe, you will receive whatever you ask for in prayer."

Jesus shared with them that through faith and words there is great power. He pointed to the power of prayer.

Remember, speaking can only be done on the exhale. Words come out from the breath: "In the beginning was the Word, and the Word was with God, and the Word was God." (John 1:1)

Additional commentary on this verse in Biblehub pointed to the meaning of the ancient Greek words this passage was originally written in:

- "Spirit" in the Greek is *pneuma* (which also means "breath")
- The Greek word *logos* is the word used to mean "the Word of YHVH made incarnate in Yeshua, Christ"
- Or philosophically neuos/mind-logic (the means of persuasion *by demonstration of the truth*)

In John 14:6, Yeshua answered, "I am the way and the truth and the life. No one comes to the Father except through me."

I hope you see how our words, ancient languages both in spirit and in logic, come together in the way of Christ. No man could say the things He said and have a consistency that is proved in fulfilling their meanings in both the spiritual, physical and intellectual Life that is consistently written, author after author, in all of the books of scripture.

It is by the Holy Spirit and of the Holy Spirit. Much that we have come to know now in the physical has only been made available by today's science, and yet the Word of YHVH has pointed to it all along.

In the earlier times the presence and potential voice of YHVH to the Hebrews was too terrifying for them.

---

18 When the people saw the thunder and lightning and heard the trumpet and saw the mountain in smoke, they trembled with fear. They stayed at a distance 19 and said to Moses, "Speak to us yourself and we will listen. But do not have YHVH speak to us or we will die." 20 Moses said to the people, "Do not be

afraid. YHVH has come to test you, so that the fear of YHVH will be with you to keep you from sinning." 21 The people remained at a distance, while Moses approached where YHVH was. (Genesis 20:18-21)

In the Book of Revelation, there is a similar account of when He spoke: "From the throne came flashes of lightning, rumblings and peals of thunder..." (Rev. 4:5a)

Again, my curiosity sparked to life. If there is lightning and thunder at times when YHVH speaks, what is lightning made of?

I got my answer from an article for students "How is Lightening Made?" 8.19.04 Nasa.gov. Their website said that cold air has ice crystals, and warm air has water droplets. The crystals and water droplets rub against each other and cause friction and static electricity that generates into the lightning bolt.

I was so excited!.

Lightning was made from two different forms of *water* reacting by rubbing against one another. The motion of the waters create such an energy that it tears apart the air and splits molecules releasing nitrogen.

Then it goes on into another life form.

Nitrogen looks for something to connect to, and when it connects with oxygen, it becomes a nitrate. As it rains, the captured nitrate dissolves into the water droplets which feed the Earth with this heavenly fertilizer.

The nitrate can be absorbed through the roots of plants. This vital nutrient enters the cells of every living organism on earth. Satellites have found that there are forty lightning strikes every second, and over three million in a day. Lightning is five times hotter than the surface of the sun and is only the thickness of a thumb.

Additional references in the Bible note YHVH speaking from both the Old and New Testament in parallel to each other:

In Revelation 1:15, from John's account, "His feet were like bronze glowing in a furnace, and his voice was like the sound of rushing waters.

In Ezekiel 43:2, from Ezekiel's account, "...and I saw the glory of the God of Israel coming from the east. His voice was like the roar of rushing waters, and the land was radiant with his glory."

Remember how our exhaled breath has water as a component? The thought of the power of YHVH's exhaled breath is staggering as we hear man's description of it. YHVH's words have been for us: "All Scripture is breathed out by YHVH and profitable for teaching, for reproof, for correction, and for training in righteousness..." (2 Timothy 3:16)

It is for our *good*.

∽

The first one to speak against man was Satan himself. Satan used words to introduce the first insecurity and led mankind to sin. Simply translated in the NLT: "Now the serpent was the shrewdest of all the creatures the Lord God had made. 'Really?' he asked the woman. 'Did God really say you must not eat any of the fruit in the garden?'" (Genesis 3:1)

Do you hear the insecurity instilled in doubt? Doubt comes from a root of insecurity.

Satan then introduced inferiority. "'You won't die!' the serpent hissed. 'God knows that your eyes will be opened when you eat it. You will become just like God, knowing everything, both good and evil.'" Even the hiss breathes out an exhale of lies.

Adam and Eve were already created in YHVH's image, free from sin. They were walking in the life of love and grace.

Satan introduced sin by using insecurity and inferiority. (*Satan's Dirty Little Secret*, Steve Foss) These are two main roots to many of our negative behaviors.

We get a good picture of the truth of Satan in John 8:44 where

Jesus says that there is *no truth* in him: "When he lies it is consistent with his character for he is a liar and the father of all lies."

Out of the root of inferiority bloomed the desire for superiority. After the example of Cain feeling inferior to Abel. Thanks to his jealousy over God's pleasure in Abel's offering over his own, Cain murdered his brother.

By this lie of their true identity in grace, and having been allowed to eat from the Tree of Life without having to know the difference between good and evil, they instead took from the tree of the Knowledge of Good and Evil. In that knowledge, sin abounds, and there is death. By their disobedience, the plantings of insecurity and doubt grew into sin as they let go of the words of YHVH.

∽

In another big example of insecurity, the people of Babel began to build a tower for themselves to the heavens. They wanted to make a name for themselves.

In Genesis 11:4-9, YHVH comes to look at what they are building and says in verses 6 and 7, "If as one people *speaking the same language* they have begun to do this, then nothing they plan to do will be impossible for them. 7 Come, let us go down and confuse their language so they will not understand each other." (Emphasis added)

YHVH knows the power of language and words, and from that point He gave them multiple languages to stop them so they could no longer work together to accomplish anything they wanted. From there He scattered them over the face of the whole Earth. Genesis 11:8

After Yeshua's death and resurrection, we see the power of language and words given back to man by His Spirit for good: The Holy Spirit came and everyone present was filled with the Holy Spirit and began speaking in other languages as the Holy Spirit gave them this ability. (Acts 2:4)

It says in Ephesians 6, as the armor of God is described, that He also gives us a weapon: the Sword of the Spirit, which is the *word* of YHVH. Paul goes on to instruct in the power of prayer in the Spirit in verse 18: "And pray in the Spirit on all occasions with all kinds of prayers and requests. With this in mind, be alert and always keep on praying for all the Lord's people."

This not only makes us armed but *dangerous*. The breath in our words, the life of breath poured into us by YHVH in the physical creation of who we are and in the spiritual, gives great power to our spoken words. Especially powerful are those words when they are spoken in the tongues of His Spirit.

CHAPTER SEVEN
WHAT WORDS CAN DO

THE INCREDIBLE POWER

From the beginning of life, YHVH started with naming us. Names are an identity, and they build a *relationship* in the knowing of one's name. The importance and power of a name is described in Acts 2:21: "And anyone who calls on the Name of the Lord will be saved." We were told to call on His Name.

I am going to be bold here. In most of the old Testament translations, you see LORD in place of what was originally YHVH. LORD is a position and not a name. The Word speaks of the Name! Why do you think YHVH was replaced in most texts?

When we recognize the Name of YHVH/Yahweh, we can then understand the power of the Name Yeshua. This is why much of my Bible references I have inserted the Names YHVH and Yeshua. I believe it is time to use His Name, His true Name. We are promised much when we do.

The angel appeared and told Mary and Joseph before He was born, that they were to call Him Yeshua. In Hebrew, Yeshua means "Yah saves/delivers." (*Hebrew Streams*, "The Hebrew Meaning of 'Jesus'")

We often don't see ourselves as YHVH sees us. He knows us and calls us by name. Sometimes Satan's lies and influence can ruin our view of ourselves , or we just don't believe the way YHVH sees us.

In Genesis 17, YHVH changed Abram's name to Abraham, blessed him, and established him as the father of many nations. In that encounter, Abraham fell down in reverence.

Sometimes an encounter that is so strong with YHVH and His Spirit, can make us fall down. Or sometimes we stop where we are and worship like Jacob did when YHVH told him he was now blessed and would no longer be called Jacob, but Israel, in Genesis 35. YHVH saw them differently than they saw themselves, so much so that He changed their names to help them fit how He was seeing them and blessing them.

Gideon had been threshing and was hiding grain in the bottom of a winepress because the Midianites had been taking all that belonged to the Israelites. In Judges 6, an angel of YHVH appeared to Gideon and said, "Mighty hero, YHVH is with you!"

Gideon didn't see himself at all like a mighty hero, but YHVH did. The angel told Gideon that he would rescue Israel. Gideon tried to argue by saying he came from the weakest clan of his entire tribe and that he was the weakest one in his entire family.

YHVH continued to help Gideon believe in who he was through Him. Gideon asked for proof of the things Yahweh/YHVH was telling him. He laid a sheepskin on the ground and asked God to have only the sheepskin be wet in the morning. Sure enough, the next morning, it was wet, and everything around it was dry.

Gideon still wasn't convinced, so he asked YHVH to keep the fleece dry and make everything else around it wet the next morning. Again, YHVH showed his power, and Gideon was convinced.

As the Spirit of YHVH came on Gideon, he got up in the night and broke his father's idols. This wild and rebellious act built him up in the way of becoming a bold and courageous person in front of the people who had heard about what he had done.

Later, YHVH whittled down the army of people that were to fight with Gideon to a ridiculously low and dangerous number. Being armed with so few would prove YHVH's strength, not theirs. Gideon was nervous about attacking, so YHVH said if Gideon needed more confidence, he should go and sneak into the camp of the enemy before the attack and hear for himself what they were saying.

As Gideon and another man went in, they heard a conversation in the tent of their enemy. They were discussing a dream that one had as the other one interpreted it. It was about the army of Gideon defeating them. Here, YHVH provided prophecy and interpretation out of the lips of Gideon's enemies, proving that YHVH was going to do this great thing.

YHVH then had Gideon and his small army carry jars with them and hide their torches inside as they approached the camp of the enemy. At YHVH/Yahweh's command, they were to throw down their clay jars, breaking them to the ground and blow their horns.

This was a large step of faith on their part, but YHVH had provided His proof. They were obedient, and YHVH defeated the Midianites as they turned on themselves and killed each other. We see YHVH's grace to Gideon to help him see who he was and how YHVH saw him, so much so that YHVH was able to use him in great ways.

Sometimes we don't see others the way that YHVH sees them. In 1 Samuel 16, YHVH tells Samuel to go and find Jesse and anoint one of his sons to be His new king.

Upon his arrival, Samuel asks Jesse to bring out his sons. As Jesse brings out the first one, even Samuel thinks, "Surely this is the LORD's anointed." But he wasn't.

They went through the seven sons that were there, and not one of them was the one God said to anoint. So Samuel asks if Jesse has any other sons and learns that the youngest is still out watching the sheep. Soon little David comes in, the eighth son, and Samuel sees him as ruddy, handsome, and with pleasant eyes.

YHVH tells Samuel that this is the one. Little David stands there among all of his big brothers and is anointed. The Spirit of YHVH comes on him from that day forward.

Before David's selection, YHVH spoke to Samuel in 1 Samuel 16:7: "But YHVH said to Samuel, 'Don't judge by his appearance or height, for I have rejected him. YHVH doesn't make decisions the way you do! People judge by outward appearance, but YHVH looks at a person's thoughts and intentions.'"

∼

Even Mary didn't see herself as YHVH saw her. When the angel appeared to Mary in Luke 1:28, the angel said, "'Greetings, favored woman! The Lord is with you!' 29 Confused and disturbed, Mary tried to think what the angel could mean. 30 'Don't be frightened, Mary,' the angel told her, 'for YHVH has decided to bless you!'"

Mary was probably wondering what there could possibly be about her to warrant such favor. Maybe she didn't feel that the Lord was with her, but she knew who YHVH was, and she believed and asked the angel how it would happen.

∼

We know a lot about ourselves. We often see our weaknesses and our faults and let those define us. We put ourselves down and often feel unworthy or unable to be used, loved, or have the freedom to approach the Creator. Satan likes to use these lies to keep us from the Creator/YHVH, but this isn't the way YHVH sees us.

Satan is known as the Accuser. Your negative thoughts about yourself are the accusations of the Enemy and his evil spirits.

Romans 8:1 says, "So now there is no condemnation for those who belong to Christ." The Creator/YHVH isn't condemning as an accuser does, but He sees you in love, and the good He has given you through coming as a Son in Yeshua. He created you to be with Him, and He made an always-open way through Yeshua's sacrifice.

As Ephesians 3:12 says, "In him and through faith in him we may approach YHVH with freedom and confidence." Think of the freedom given to the second dove after the first dove was sacrificed.

Look at the word "confidence." Confidence is not present when we look at our faults and our weakness. Confidence comes in seeing ourselves the way YHVH sees us through the perfection of Yeshua. It comes by knowing that He loves us so much that He sent His only son to be the way to perfect us.

Our confidence is in Him and Him in us. He desires our presence and our relationship with Him and wants us to see ourselves the way He sees us so that we can come to Him in confidence.

Mary's confidence was in YHVH.

As YHVH spoke positive things for people in the Bible, they began to walk and live in the way He saw them, and their lives changed. Some of us have heard harsh things said about us or to us. If negative words about yourself afflict your mind, write down the opposite of that word. The bad is not of YHVH, because YHVH is good.

The opposite word, which is good, would be of YHVH. Start seeing yourself in the way YHVH sees you, and be confident that He loves you and wants you to come to Him freely and confidently. He sees you in that good way through the sacrifice of Yeshua's blood cleansing you from everything bad. You are free!

Through these biblical examples, we see that there is great power in words. "The tongue has the power of life and death, and those who love it will eat its fruit." (Proverbs 18:21)

This is sobering. Good words can give life, and the harsh and cruel words can cause death.

I know when I speak well to someone, they improve. Also, they in turn begin to speak well of themselves and others. Likewise, if I am negative or harsh or aggressive with my words, the other person often reacts back to me in the same way. We do eat the fruit of what we put out.

I saw this in the physical when my father-in-law was nearing death. He came from a different country, and for his last nine years, he lived in America.

The hospice nurse asked if there were other family members who could come, and we said they were too far away. She recommended that we call them and ask them to call and talk to him if they were able to do so. My former father-in-law was unable to speak anymore, and he was no longer opening his eyes, but he could still hear.

One after the other, his brothers, sister, and children called. I knelt at his bedside holding the phone to his ear. As the calls came, he began to move slightly, nod, and even smile at some of the words being said to him.

He had some relationships that had grown distant, and one of his family members hadn't spoken with him in seventeen years. He got a phone call from her and heard her voice. His eyes opened, and I could see the light in his eyes. He was tired after all of it, but he was peaceful and content.

I went to see him the following morning, unsure how much further he would have declined. When I got there, not only was he awake, but he was sitting in a chair, talking and wanting food. I was stunned!

I found a note from the hospice nurse that said my father-in-law was up with her and she had given him breakfast, that he was watching the re-run of the Royal Wedding, and that he'd recited The Lord's Prayer with them when they said it on the television.

This was such palpable evidence of the power of words; they brought life. He wasn't able to see these people, but he listened to them over the phone as they told him they loved him. The doctors and hospice had previously said he would be gone in 48 hours, but this event helped to add another month to his life.

When we speak well of people and encourage them, it is a good fruit for them. Likewise, it makes it easy for the other person to respond back in a kind manner.

After my father-in-law's comeback, he started to tell all of us that he loved us and that we were never to forget it. He said that he loved all of the people that weren't able to be there, too. He had never outwardly spoken like that to us before.

This left us with so much to hold onto now that he's gone. It was a kind of fruit that does not go away. Because of what he received, he had to give to others. The nurses' kind words hadn't done it. The power of the words came from people he had intimate relationships with.

When we are mean or say hurtful things, we often receive the same kinds of words in response. It cuts and hurts and handicaps us from growing into the good way God created us, and we both walk away wounded and hurt. Even our tone of voice and the *way* we say things can hurt and harm people.

I used to be a master of using sarcasm. I could say what I wanted without really saying the exact words. This phrase says it so well: "Sarcasm... because beating the crap out of people is illegal."

Sarcasm really is like that. Those words and attitude beat a person down. Our words, which come from our breath, are powerful because YHVH breathed life in us. We need to truly comprehend the way God made us and that His plan for us was to be life-giving and a help. The purpose for us in this is huge!

Spewed, negative words, the division that occurs over attitudes, disdain, and unforgiveness without considering another and the death spoken in perversion, self-centered and self-seeking ways is destroying homes, hearts of children, and people all over. Hearing the words, "I'm sorry" is like a salve on a wound. "I forgive you" marks the restoration of the relationship. Saying "I love you" gives so much value and strengthens relationships.

Saying "I love you" for the first time is often the beginning of a new life between a man and woman. Hearing it from a parent is as foundationally comforting as having been held safely and close on their lap.

These words reach us deeply.

The reason for it is all part of the way we are created. Our purpose at this time on Earth is great. There is only one you, and only you know the people that you know, go to the places that you go, and can give life from your lips as you speak well into others. No one else has your voice. Your voice comes from the breath of the life within you.

～

One perfect example of living in love is shown in Psalm 145:8, where it says that Yahweh is merciful and compassionate, slow to get angry and filled with unfailing love.

If we are living in love, then our words come from that place and are life-giving—words of mercy, compassion, patience, and unfailing love.

Love, when expressed in the intimate, physical way between a man and woman, is the very place of where a physical life is created. God shows us examples in the physical and spiritual ways of His true heart: love and life and intimacy and the power accompanying them.

He has said that our words can bring life or death. Our words are personal and intimate and reach us in spiritual and emotional ways that can help or hurt, give life or death.

Think of the way you talk to people in your life. What are your words doing? Are they out of love? A good check-up can be found in 1 Corinthians 13:4-7:

> Love is patient, love is kind. It does not envy, it does not boast, it is not proud. 5 It does not dishonor others, it is not self-seeking, it is not easily angered, it keeps no record of wrongs. 6 Love does not delight in evil but rejoices with the truth. 7 It always protects, always trusts, always hopes, always perseveres.

How do you talk to yourself? Are you running yourself down? Some motivational speakers teach positive affirmations, which means telling yourself good things about yourself. These words help us to do better.

When you understand the way you are created, with the power of breath and spirit from the Creator/YHVH Himself, and that you are the very essence of Him and Heaven, you can see why there is so much power to it and why you should see yourself the way God sees you. "Love does not delight in evil, but rejoices in truth!" (1 Corinthians 13:6)

The power of YHVH's words are living and active and precise. YHVH does not exaggerate or underestimate. His words are so powerful that it transforms lives. It creates a new life and spirit inside:

> "For the word of YHVH is living and active. Sharper than any double-edged sword, it penetrates even to dividing soul and spirit, joints and marrow; it judges the thoughts and attitudes of the heart." (Hebrews 4:12)

> "In his right hand he held seven stars, and out of his mouth came a sharp double-edged sword. His face was like the sun shining in all its brilliance." (Revelation 1:16)

Satan is called a liar and Father of all Lies. There is no truth in him. No good word. Someone once said that in a way, negative words are the worship language of Hell. They destroy and kill and there is no good fruit.

Yeshua cursed the fig tree for having no fruit, stopping its life as it shriveled and dried up. The tree had not been fulfilling its purpose. This is not meant to be a place of condemnation for you but rather a place of becoming aware and persevering. It is a light shining on the darkness of the Enemy.

Pray against the words of the Enemy, and pray in the power of YHVH's truth of love, purpose, and His vision of you and those you know. This week, notice any negative thoughts that come against you about yourself. Write the opposite of that thought which is the positive.

Yeshua wants you to know His love, His power and His Spirit in you to be what He has made you to be through Him. Keep your list of positives, and praise Him for seeing you in those ways and giving you those things. The positives are pluses, and a plus is an addition, and that addition is the provision and giving of YHVH to you. Receive what He is giving you.

You're on the path of your identity with the Creator!

CHAPTER EIGHT
THE POWER

In John 11:43-44, Yeshua "called out in a loud voice" for Lazarus to come out of the grave, and by Yeshua's voice and command, Lazarus was raised from the dead in front of a crowd.

Yeshua states that He knew what Yahweh would do. He could have raised Lazerus in a quiet way, but He chose to do it this way so that they too, might believe.

Yeshua shows the power of His words in Mark 4:39: "When Jesus woke up, he rebuked the wind and said to the waves, 'Silence! Be still!' Suddenly the wind stopped, and there was a great calm."

These examples show Yeshua *conquering* storms and death by His words. Take this to heart and mind. His words also helped others to believe as they heard him speak and saw the results of what happened by what he *said*.

We see peace, and we see life and freedom. In His presence dwell such things. When we come to Him in prayer or read His Word, this is what pours from His breath into our lives.

Numbers 20:1-12 is a powerful illustration of Yahweh's instruction to Moses about speaking, the power of words, and Yahweh's intention to show their power. The people were thirsty and needed water. They complained to Moses, and Aaron and said to Moses, "You brought us out here to die?"

Moses went to Yahweh/YHVH, who told him to take the stick and to *speak* to the rock and water would come out from it. When Moses returned to the angry people who had just spoken to him in complaining and aggression, he responded in anger and, in self-righteous frustration said, "Listen you rebels, *must we* bring you water out of this rock?"

Moses' words took ownership of the act of providing. Moses then struck the rock not once, but twice with his staff instead of speaking to it as Yahweh had commanded, and still the water gushed out of the rock. This was the act that kept Moses from seeing the Promised Land:

---

12 But YHVH said to Moses and Aaron, "Because you did not trust in me enough to honor me as holy in the sight of the Israelites, you will not bring this community into the land I give them." 13 These were the waters of Meribah,[a] where the Israelites quarreled with YHVH and where he showed himself holy among them. (Numbers 20:12-13 NIV)

Moses and Aaron, who had done so much that was great, had not done it of their own works or might, but through Him through words and their obedience. And so they no longer received the rest of what YHVH was giving: the Promised Land.

Greater yet, beyond the knowledge of the Israelites and Moses, is the representation of the spiritual in the event. YHVH showed the strength and power of words rather than might.

He also showed His mercy and His provision, even in our failures. The water still flowed from the rock to save their lives, while they were yet sinners. God showed that as Christ is the rock, His living water pours out to us through His Spirit and gives us life in the spiritual and eternal. It is a pouring out of His grace—provision for life that we did not earn but were given because we are loved.

> "...and all drank the same spiritual drink; for they drank from the spiritual Rock that followed them, and the Rock was Christ." (1 Corinthians 10:4)

As Yeshua hung on the cross, beaten and pierced, He still offered forgiveness and everlasting life as blood and water poured out from His side.

> "Yeshua answered, 'It is written: "Man does not live on bread alone, but on every word that comes from the mouth of God.""'" (Matthew 4:4)

> In the beginning was the Word, and the Word was with God, and the Word was God. 2He was with God in the beginning. 3Through him all things were made; without him nothing was made that has been made. 4In him was life, and that life was the light of men. 5The light shines in the darkness, but the darkness has not understood[a] it. (John 1:1-5)

I have to admit that all of this was dark to me until His Spirit showed me the dove-like breath and captured my thoughts and consumed my curiosity. If not for that, I would not have found this incredible foundation with Yahweh.

I can't take a single word of credit for it except that I sat down with all of the puzzle pieces He was handing me and put together the picture He had already created from the beginning.

Here's another piece from John 8:20-21: "Someone told him, 'Your mother and brothers are standing outside, wanting to see you.' ²¹ He replied, 'My mother and brothers are those who hear God's word and put it into practice.'"

Here we see the pieces fitting together. We see the relationships in Christ. We become part of an intimate family where words are life. We see here that it is through God's Word and putting it into practice.

> "For the one whom God has sent speaks the words of God, for God gives the Spirit/Ruah without limit." (John 3:34)

Here are more scriptures to take to heart as you move forward in the knowledge and wisdom of what YHVH has given you:

> Let your speech always be gracious, seasoned with salt, so that you may know how to ought to answer each person. (Colossians 4:6)

> The heart of the wise teaches his mouth, and adds learning to his lips. Pleasant words are like a honeycomb, sweetness to the soul and health to the bones. (Proverbs 16:23-24 NKJV)

> A gentle answer turns away wrath, but a harsh word stirs up anger. (Proverbs 15:1)

> The good person out of his good treasure brings forth good, and the evil person out of his evil treasure brings forth evil. 36 I tell you, on the day of judgment people will give account for every careless word they speak, 37 for by your words you will be justified, and by your words you will be condemned." (Matthew 12:35-36)

The power of words is life. Words can live for all time.

When we think of great people, we think of the things that they said. We often quote them. Their words are as alive today as they were then. When the belongings of these great people decay or rot away, their words live on vibrant and strong.

It is the words that continue; the stories told or written and remembered. We repeat words said by family members long since passed on, and their words persist.

When I was growing up, our elementary school did an experiment each year for the twelve-year-olds: we grew bean plants from seeds. We watered our plants and kept them by the sunlight.

But we also separated the plants and placed half on one side of the room and the other half on the other side of the room. On one side, we were told that we could "talk" in kind voices and positive words to the plants. On the other side of the room we could talk in mean voices and use ridiculing and criticizing words.

We got to witness the effect of words on plants. The ones that received good words grew taller, stronger, and fuller. The plants that got the negative talk grew small, straggly, and weak. I remember this vividly.

Of course, as kids do, some tried to sabotage the process by speaking meanly to the plants that were to receive the good, so I don't think the experiment continued much longer.

A friend of mine is an organic gardener. Her plants are truly the largest, strongest, and healthiest plants I have ever seen or transplanted. Her garden beds are well tended-to and watered.

The one thing that I see her do differently from other gardeners is that she plays music through speakers mounted on the outside of her home as she gardens all day. The station she listens to plays Christian music. Her plants are drenched in this music with worshipful words of YHVH.

You may think this sounds farfetched, but I have witnessed it. I am an avid gardener myself and have spent many years around plants, nurseries, and other growers. Her plants are unlike any I have ever seen.

In fact, I had some of her tomato plants in a pot by the door of my home. I received a large bouquet of flowers from a high-end florist and garden center, and the delivery driver raved about the tomato plants being the most remarkable she had ever seen. Years ago I would hear about elder women with amazing houseplants about how they "talk to their plants."

I have also seen kind, purposeful words spoken to people and the strength and encouragement and growth that those words have on people. Even as infants, kind words soothe and calm. Pets recognize kind words and are drawn near, but at angry words, they may run and cower.

YHVH is inviting us to talk to Him as He speaks to us in love. He is gentle and has given you the essence of Himself in being created in His image. Your prayers, your words, and your thoughts matter to Him, and He wants them to matter to you, too. He also wants you to know His words to you. Knowing them helps you know Him.

∽

There are times when I long to know YHVH so much more that I can hardly stand it. Reading the Bible helps so much. I have also learned to be quiet and recognize His voice. It is a matter of opening up ourselves to believe it, receive it, and really listen.

Sometimes He speaks in situations or things happening that only He could have planned. Like we have learned, communication doesn't always come through words alone.

At times, I *need* to be near YHVH in relationship or communion. Psalm 42:1 expresses this well: "For the director of music. A maskil of the Sons of Korah. As the deer pants for streams of water, so my soul pants for you, O God."

I saw this in real life last fall. I was on my way to visit someone at a facility where she was recovering from knee replacement surgery. The campus of the facility sat deep in the woods on a tall hillside high above the Minnesota River.

I saw a deer with antlers standing near the drive that we were on. He stood with his mouth open and panting. I had never seen a deer do this before. That verse came to mind as my own soul recognized that current desire I was experiencing. The deer didn't have much farther to go for to reach a stream. Neither did I.

I had been writing this book but had stopped because I felt so empty and "dry." When I went to my computer that night after having seen the deer and identifying with the scripture verse of my own soul panting for the water, I found an e-mail from another writer and Bible teacher whom I greatly admire.

She had blogged to "authors." I had never known her to address so narrow an audience. She encouraged and uplifted in the importance of continuing on to write, to go to YHVH in times of dryness and to spend time with Him.

This was a way of YHVH communicating to me. He knew my longing and showed me that He knew. I wept my own streams as I drew near to Him, knowing how intimately He knew me and provided for me. From there I was able to go on.

Not all of my words and conversations with YHVH have been serious or weighty in neediness. Sometimes I just plain have fun with Him. I will laugh when He boldly shows me something to the point where He's showing off. Other times I'm just living out my day.

One morning after a bath, I was getting ready in front of the mirror. I had spent time praising and singing while in the bathtub and thanking Him again and again that He let me live in a time when I can turn a handle and warm, clean water pours out of the faucet.

Looking in the mirror, I saw another hair on my chin that I was going to have to tweeze. I said out loud to Him, "So, what are we going to do about this?"

I was halfway hoping He'd give me a miraculous removal of the offenders.

Instead, He said, "I had one, too."

I laughed so hard. Yes, by all accounts, I believe Yeshua had a beard.

Yeshua is funny. We are created in His image. We have a sense of humor. Where did you think it came from?

A prayer:

> Yahweh, may our words grow more frequently toward You during our days. Let us talk with You from a place of intimacy. Fully remove any words that are not of You that we think about ourselves and replace them with who You are in us.
>
> When we talk to others, let our words encourage, strengthen, comfort, and love. Let them be words of life. In Yeshua's Name, Amen.

Prayer brings us into relationship. We talk about everything with our best friends. Yeshua has called us friends. Let's talk with Him as a friend.

No longer do I call you servants, for the servant does not know what his master is doing; but I have called you friends, for all that I have heard from my Father I have made known to you. (John 15:15

CHAPTER NINE
RELATIONAL PRAYER

A FRIEND ALWAYS READY TO LISTEN

Prayer is your open invitation for as long as you are breathing. You can show up any day and any way for as often and as long as you want. The sooner I show up, the better it is for me. YHVH is always there and ready. I just need to notice and open up myself to Him.

Some days I can go almost all day just interacting with Him and taking in all that He is. Other days, when I am busy or feeling self-sufficient, I can lay down at night and think, "Wow, I really missed you today, YHVH." He was there, but I wasn't. My eyes were more inward or outward and not upward.

Sometimes when worries weighed so heavily on me, it was all I could do to peel my eyes off of what was in front of me and look to the One that was and is and will be. I could almost feel my eyeballs, as if they weighed as much as stones, dry in their sockets as I forced them from looking down at my problems to looking up to His promises and hope. I knew what I needed to do, but it was so hard.

Graham Cooke, a pastor, speaker and author was talking about Creator and said about Him that if you are in Him, then so are your problems.

What a relief that is. When the Creator is right there in the midst of it all, the problems suddenly look insignificant compared to Who He is. He wants to give us peace.

The Creator has much to give to us. It is to His glory when He gives. He is communicating back in so many ways. We have forgotten that. Our ancestors used to see Him in everything. We only need to open ourselves up to look and be aware and listen.

"'Come to me, all of you who are weary and carry heavy burdens, and I will give you rest.'" (Matthew 11:28)

"For I will satisfy the weary soul, and every languishing soul I will replenish." (Jeremiah 31:25)

He loves you so much that He wants you to be well and to have rest. When turmoil swirls around us and we are rested or refreshed in spite of it, it speaks of Him.

Only He can do such things for us. It bewilders onlookers. But it is a reality for those who walk through their days looking up to Him each day. Being in prayer keeps up the relationship.

Relationships are built on trust, and trust comes from spending time in each other's presence.

"So I say to you: Ask and it will be given to you; seek and you will find; knock and the door will be opened to you." (Luke 11:9 NKJ)

"You will seek me and find me when you seek me with all your heart." (Jeremiah 29:13)

These are promises. He knows the difference between half-hearted seeking and seeking Him with your whole heart. When we seek or go to Him with our whole heart, with our eyes wide open looking for Him, He is found. It is a fullness of honesty.

He says to knock on the door and it will be opened. We don't just approach the door and stand there, hoping He will open it up to us. We need to participate. We need to knock. Pray. Talk. It's called coming into His presence.

I have known people who are angry, but they go honestly to Yahweh while being angry and tell Him that they are. They are comfortable in their relationship because they spend time in His presence.

Wholeheartedness is the fullness or wholeness of all that we are, being directed fully towards Him. It isn't going to Him with thoughts like, "He's probably not listening" or "He probably doesn't care."

Those are still inner thoughts to yourself and not to Him. You are better to say, "Show me You" or " Let me know You are here with me" or "Don't let me miss You."

This demonstrates more fullness of heart. Believe you are asking things that He can do. This takes faith. He loves to build your faith.

Your faith is built on what He has done or will do. Look to the Bible and all He has done. These are faith-builders. Start talking to Him about it. I've asked Him to do for me like He did for David or to strengthen me like Joshua.

There are so many ways to see Yahweh's love, compassion, mercy, and grace. This is what He does and who He is. He wants to give to you like this. This is the exchange of intimacy and relationship.

Here is some of what He does when you come to Him as you are:

- The broken are mended.
- The forsaken find faithfulness.
- The troubled have peace.
- The sinners are forgiven.
- The weary get rest.
- The lowly are lifted.
- The empty are filled.
- The weak find strength.
- The parched are refreshed.
- The grieving are comforted.

"You make known to me the path of life; in your presence there is fullness of joy; at your right hand are pleasures forevermore." (Psalm 16:11)

These things come out of being in His presence. Talk with Him, be with Him, and let go of the bad so He can give you what He has instead.

There is joy in His presence. There are pleasures of living with Him forever.

---

15 If you love me, you will obey what I command. 16And I will ask the Father, and he will give you another Counselor to be with you forever— 17 the Spirit of truth. The world cannot accept him, because it neither sees him nor knows him. But you know him, for he lives with you and will be in you. 18 I will not leave you as orphans; I will come to you. 19 Before long, the world will not see me anymore, but you will see me. Because I live, you also will live. 20 On that day you will realize that I am in my Father, and you are in me, and I am in you. 21 Whoever has my commands and obeys them, he is the one who loves me. He who loves me will be loved by my

Father, and I too will love him and show myself to him. (John 14:15-21)

Opening up yourself to His presence comes in a variety of ways. Some people talk to Yahweh in a posture of a bowed head and folded hands. It is a way to focus on Him by concentrating and closing out distractions.

Our ancestors opened their hands with palms up as in the posture of receiving and opening themselves up. Some people bow down low to the floor or kneel, grounding and humbling themselves in a lowly position. Some people like to keep their eyes open.

There are as many ways to come into His presence as there are things to say. It's individual, and sometimes it's situational. Your ability to focus on Him and be open to Him is the key.

If His presence can't be ignored then it's time to talk to Him or listen to Him. He has your attention. Even if it's saying to Him "That sunset is amazing! Thank you."

The more you notice Him in the big things, the more your vision sharpens for the smaller things. He heightens your sensitivity the more you interact with Him.

It took a while for me to understand what my children's babble meant and to interpret their cries. But now that my son is seven, I can recognize the first note out of his throat if he's been hurt, even among a crowd of kids.

From my older daughters' first "hello" over the phone, I can tell if they are worried or anxious or happy or enthused. It comes from constantly interacting with them in all kinds of ways.

Intimate relationships require knowing each other.

YHVH desires you to know Him. To know He keeps His promises, to know He loves you and gives you peace, to know He is the source of everything you need. The more you talk to Him, the more you recognize Him and His ways.

The disciples asked Yeshua how they should pray, and he demonstrated the Lord's Prayer for them. It is a prayer that comes from a place of surrender. It is a place where you are acknowledging that you can do nothing apart from Him.

Some people say it often during church services, and it may have become automatic for them. Taking it bit by bit reveals a much greater depth to it. Think of tree roots that reach deeper into the soil for water.

We need to reach deeper into His Word to help us stand and flourish without being affected by harsh conditions. A deeper faith and deeper understanding of Him helps you to survive the harder times.

Like the woman that survived the fires of Colorado Springs, she had a deep faith and knew her LORD and could stand there, hot, dirty, and having just lost her home and say, "I know something good will come from this. God is good." She knew Him.

Yeshua answers them starting in Matthew 6:9 with this prayer: **"Our father who is in heaven."** This is key!

He is opening the prayer with relationship. Not only is the relationship between you and Yahweh the Father, but it is between you and Yeshua as you say with Him, "Our Father."

Let's look at that first line and follow the many trails that lead to that place of relationship to our father in heaven. Yeshua also points to the family relationship with Him when He says in Matthew 12:49, "Here are my mother and my brothers."

"The Spirit himself testifies with our spirit that we are God's children. 17 Now if we are children, then we are heirs—heirs of God and co-heirs with Christ, if indeed we share in his sufferings in order that we may also share in his glory." (Romans 8:16-17)

Yeshua wants us to know this and start out in prayer as a beloved child. It's a great way to start a conversation feeling like this. To know that you are a co-heir with Yeshua to the inheritance of all that is in Heaven and of YHVH's.

Our relationship with Yeshua is not only as a brother and co-heir but also as a friend.

Yeshua calls us His friend. As the old hymn says, "What a friend I have in Jesus."

Here are examples of mentions of relationships and the reasons why:

"This is the account of Noah. Noah was a righteous man, blameless among the people of his time, and he walked with YHVH." (Genesis 6:9)

Walking with God is a daily routine. It means being with Him everywhere you go. It made Noah righteous because he walked in YHVH's righteousness.

"And the scripture was fulfilled that says, 'Abraham believed YHVH, and it was credited to him as righteousness,' and he was called Yahweh's friend." (James 2:23)

Abraham believed what YHVH told him and did what He told him to do. He was obedient. That is faith: believing and obeying.

He didn't oppose Yahweh or question, but went with Him out of faith that Yahweh cared about him. That is friendship.

When my girlfriend asks me to meet her for coffee, I say, "Okay." I don't ask her why or say I don't want to or wonder if she's a friend. A friend gets up and goes and will do what they can to be with another friend. I know she's there for me and cares about me, and I enjoy being with her.

> "YHVH would speak to Moses face to face, as a man speaks with his friend. Then Moses would return to the camp, but his young aide Joshua son of Nun did not leave the tent." (Exodus 33:11)

YHVH talked to Moses, and Moses responded back. They dialogued back and forth.

> "After removing Saul, he made David their king. He testified concerning him: 'I have found David son of Jesse a man after my own heart; he will do everything I want him to do.'" (Acts 13:22)

This is another thing YHVH looks for: someone who will do what He asks. Noah did it by building the ark. Abraham did it by leaving his father's tent and being willing to sacrifice Isaac, but he continued to believe that no matter what, YHVH Himself would provide the sacrifice. Moses did what YHVH said most of the time, too.

But David was said to be willing to do everything YHVH wanted him to do. That is the heart of relationship and friendship and a strong faith which comes down to trust, respect and love.

To do those things that they did, one has to listen to YHVH. Listening is half of communing. Loving YHVH fully makes it easier to obey Him. It was easier to honor my parents and do what they asked of me when they spoke out of a loving relationship.

Some people grow up with parents who didn't provide an environment that made obedience something that they wanted to do. This can hinder relationships and trust and ruin the understanding of love.

For them, trust is a harder thing to achieve in a relationship with the Creator/YHVH as a Father, but spending time in His word and understanding the faithful and good love of YHVH starts to break down those walls that keep one from trusting and will gently lead us to a place of a loving and willing obedience and relationship if we let Him.

Psalms is full of prayers and praises. A friend described times of lamenting as stumbling around in the forest and continuing to walk until you finally come out into the light.

David is shown to write out his prayers and praises in ways that resemble this. He often starts out with great needs or fears or concerns.

As he is praying these things, you continually see him come to the place of praise. He works his way through the woods and out into the light.

He turns his eyes away from his circumstances and back to the goodness and power of YHVH. He reaches the place of praising and trusting in Him no matter what is happening because He knows that YHVH is good and the final outcome is about YHVH.

David's honesty and fullness of heart in sharing all parts of himself with YHVH is the kind of relationship YHVH wants from us. David got it. He talked to YHVH no matter how he was feeling because he recognized YHVH is there in every part of life. David gives excellent examples of what it is like to commune. "YHVH is a good Father."

The next incredible portion to this prayer, when spoken in Hebrew, is this: "Our Father who is in heaven is" *Avinu She bashamayim*. Do you remember how the word for Heaven is *shamayim*? The Hebrew for this section translates into "The One who is in the midst of the waters of Life."

The next part of the prayer is **"hallowed be your name."** We have talked about the importance of a name and how the name brings about relationship as well as saying who YHVH/Yahweh is. The names of Yahweh are power in themselves as you think of Him in the ways that you need Him: provider, King of kings, rock, strength, refuge, comforter, and on.

> Jehovah Jireh = *Yahweh Provides*
> Jeohovah Rophe = *I am Yahweh that Heals you*
> Jehovah Nissi = *Yahweh my banner, victory*
> Jehovah M'kaddesh = *Yahweh who makes you holy*
> Jehovah Shalom = *Yahweh of peace*
> Jehovah Tsidkenu =*Yahweh our righteousness*]
> Jehovah Rohi = *Yahweh our Shepherd*

Remember that He is holy and that the power of His name is Holy and not to be used in cursing or thoughtlessness. Knowing Him as the One seated on the throne, that He alone is pure, righteous, just, and that all things are of Him puts us in a place removing our vanities, pride, and self-righteousness.

Anything we hold up can't compete with His greatness. Our idols shatter at the mention of His name.

Here are more of His names:

> Elohim = *Strength/power*
> Elohay Kedem = *God of the Beginning*
> Elohay Mishpat = *God of Justice*
> Elohay Selichot = *God of Forgiveness*
> Elohay Marom = *God of Heights*
> Elohay Mikarov = *God Who is Near*
> Elohay Mauzi = *God of My Strength*
> El Shaddai = *God that is sufficient (God that is enough)*
> Elohay Tehilati = *God of My Praise*
> Elohay Yishi = *God of My Salvation*
> Elohim Kedoshim = *Holy God*

Elohim Chaiyim = *Living God*
El HaNe'eman = *The Faithful God*
El HaGadol = *The Great God*
El Elyon = *Most High God*
Immanu El = *God is With Us*
El Olam = *God of Eternity*

(Wikipedia, "Names of God in Judaism") (Names of God; Wellness Tool; Native Strong ARC)

The Name of God, YHVH, have the four letters that comes from the Hebrew verb "to be." YHVH is used in the Old Testament approximately 6828 times. (Theopedia.com; Yahweh)

The statement, "I Am Who I Am; I Am has sent you" declares His absolute being, the source of everything without beginning and without end.

Yeshua presents Himself as YHVH in John 8:56-59:

---

56 "Your father Abraham rejoiced at the thought of seeing my day; he saw it and was glad." 57 "You are not yet fifty years old," they said to him, "and you have seen Abraham!" 58 "Very truly I tell you," Jesus answered, "before Abraham was born, I am!"

---

13 And I will do whatever you ask in my name, so that the Son may bring glory to the Father. 14 You may ask me for anything in my name, and I will do it. (John 14:13-14)

Look at the intimacy in being allowed to call Him by name. We have different levels of acquaintance even in the allowing of people to call us by our names. We have prefixes of "Mr." or titles like "Dr." or we have birth names, Indian names, clan names.

Eventually, we have nicknames representative of the nearness of family, friends, and as familiarity arises. I have different nicknames from many different close people or groups of people, depending on who they are.

Yeshua brings us to the extreme intimacy of calling YHVH our *Abba* Father, meaning "Daddy."

Allow yourself to draw near in that kind of love through His desire to commune with you. Be present with Him. He breathed life into you; your breath and words are also dear and precious to Him as an exchange of intimacy.

It must delight Him when we call Him "Daddy." He's hallowed, but He's your hallowed Daddy. What can stand against that relationship?

Nothing. Nothing can separate you from His love.

Claim who you are in Him. You are His wonderfully created child, and He provided a life in which He wants you to have in abundant relationship with Him. He is the giver of life here and forever. Embrace this exchange and this intimate link to your Creator.

Yeshua went to the cross for your ability to be near and in a relationship as an heir of your Father/Creator. Even as a twelve-year-old, he said he was about his Father's business.

The most striking moment for me is when Yeshua cries out on the cross, "My God, My God, why have you forsaken me?"

This was when the weight of the sins of all of man and the curse on the Earth were upon him. YHVH does not inhabit sin. This was the first time Yeshua was out of relationship with His Father and forsaken because of the sin placed on him.

His relationship shifted as he took our punishment, and we hear it in his cry as he was separated from the nearness of calling God Father, or *Abba*. He still called out to God, but not in the ways of Sonship. Instead, Jesus still recognized Him as all-powerful God, Holy, and being his, but he wasn't *feeling* the relationship of Father. His cry still clangs against my ears.

I remember a time of heightened distance between my daughter and me. It was bad in ways of not connecting on the same heart level and a lack of communication to know the details of the situation.

My other daughter recognized it and shared with her sister that she needed to understand my "Lori-ness." In her wisdom, my daughter stepped away from seeing me as "Mom." This brought into light who I was as a person lessening the pain of a disapproving or misunderstanding Mom that probably seemed as if I was forsaking her. It was a painful time for both of us.

Soon, through prayer, I was able to let go of judgment and love the way YHVH does in relationship through Yeshua. YHVH's desire is relationship and in His holiness we are able to be part of that through the power of forgiveness. Forgiven and loved, we are fully free to come along side Our Father in Heaven and live with His presence and Kingdom on earth.

CHAPTER TEN
KEYS TO THE KINGDOM

"Your kingdom come, your will be done on earth as it is in heaven."

Yeshua's message was about the good news of the Kingdom of YHVH having come to Earth. By His coming and His presence with us, man got to experience firsthand His love, power, healing, hope, forgiveness, grace, kindness, gentleness, forbearance, peace, and new life after death.

He taught about what the Father is like. He said if you have seen me, you have seen the Father:

> Jesus said to him, "Have I been with you so long, and you still do not know me, Philip? Whoever has seen me has seen the Father. How can you say, 'Show us the Father'? Do you not believe that I am in the Father and the Father is in me? The words that I say to you I do not speak on my own authority, but the Father who dwells in me does his works. Believe me that I am in the Father and the Father is in me, or else believe on account of the works themselves." (John 14:9-11)

As Yeshua *spoke* YHVH's *truths*. He opened the hearts of men. People began to follow Him, watch Him, and listen to Him. They saw the miracles and heard the words and they received it and believed.

In Matthew 10:8, he instructed, "Heal the sick, raise the dead, cleanse those who have leprosy, drive out demons. Freely you have received, freely give."

"I will give you the keys of the kingdom of heaven; whatever you bind on earth will be bound in heaven, and whatever you loose on earth will be loosed in heaven." (Matthew 16:19)

Praying the Kingdom come and His will be done is a continuation of a desire to serve YHVH in this way: that YHVH will provide the power and presence of the Kingdom by His will being done.

When we pray this, we open up to be receptors of it. Freely receiving and freely giving. "His will be done" also involves our obedience, and that, too, is part of our surrender and the beginning of our rest, which is of the Kingdom.

At this time now, YHVH has provided His nearness and presence for us, and we can walk in the same strengths of the Kingdom. Not until Yeshua was the Kingdom fully available. He brought about the abundance of the Kingdom of YHVH for all who believed.

I believe this is what he meant in Matthew 11:11: "I tell you the truth: Among those born of women there has not risen anyone greater than John the Baptist; yet he who is least in the kingdom of heaven is greater than he."

The fullness of the Kingdom had not yet been realized by John the Baptist because John's death preceded Jesus' resurrection. John's life didn't portray any great miracles but rather, he believed the promise of YHVH. He lived a life of obedience and boldness. He told people to turn to YHVH baptizing them from an old life to a new life in the river waters. This wasn't a mikveh cleansing to be pure for one another, This was a cleansing from sinful ways to live right for YHVH. John lived solely for YHVH as he lived out the faith of the promise of the new life.

He dwelled in the wilderness alone until the time came for him to prepare the people for the coming of redemption, and he proclaimed that the Kingdom of Heaven had come near in Matthew 3:2.

John was the first to baptize in this way. He was the first to bring the fullness of spirit into the hearts and minds of men as they prepared for the fullness of the Savior as he immersed each person into the waters repenting from their old ways of life to a new life.

Yeshua considered that no one was born greater than John by this act of faith. The symbolism of the new birth and baptism is significant because of the testimony of Yeshua about John the Baptist and none being greater than him up to that time.

It was John who leaped within his mother's womb at the mention by Mary that the Christ child was within her. John was given the faith and knowledge of the Savior coming while within the womb.

Yet those who came after John that are even the least in the Kingdom were greater, because they lived and breathed from the fullness of the Kingdom come—Christ in us through His Spirit.

When asked by the Pharisees when the Kingdom of God would come, Jesus answered them, "The kingdom of God is not coming with signs to be observed, nor will they say, 'Look, here it is!' or 'There!' for behold, the kingdom of God is in the midst of you." (Luke 17:20-21 ESV)

"Behold" means to "fix your attention to it, to look upon it and perceive it." It is here now, and we need to notice it. Those feelings you get, like you should call someone, but you didn't and then you find out you should have? Those are the things of YHVH. They are the Kingdom around you. It is His Spirit nudging you.

Recognizing Him more in the way He communicates can be used for much good. We can grow in it. I've learned that the growing is limitless. It is up to me how much I choose to see those opportunities. They are all around us, as if saying, "Look, here we are!"

"Give us this day our daily bread"

This part of the prayer acknowledges that all we need and have comes from YHVH. It's trusting Him to provide for us as our provider. This is a kingdom key. Let's follow this back in the Word and see how this part of the prayer is layered with relational meaning with our Almighty God when we pray this. YHVH established daily provision by giving manna to the Hebrew people day after day for forty years. Each morning they had fresh manna.

He established His faithful provision and neither allowed them to question it nor allowed them to save any for the next day. Anything they tried to save went bad. They had to watch Him faithfully provide to build their faith in a daily relationship. Even still, there were failures of their faith.

Speaking our need and knowing it comes from YHVH keeps us in a daily dependence upon His presence in our lives. Again, this builds relationship, and we are speaking it in these words: "Give us this day our daily bread."

YHVH's purpose in revealing the bread as another part of His presence coincides with the traditional requirement of the tabernacle in the Old Testament. There was to be fresh bread kept in the tabernacle. The bread was called "The Bread of the Presence." 1 Samuel 21:6

YHVH goes further with this. As He came to us in Christ Yeshua, it was prophesied that He would be born in Bethlehem, and He was. In Hebrew, the name Bethlehem means "House of Bread." Micah 5:2

Matthew 1:23 reads, "Behold, the virgin shall conceive and bear a son, and they shall call his name Immanuel" (which means, God with us).

This discovery delighted me. Yeshua was God being present with us— the "Bread of the Presence." And there's more:

The priests were the only ones allowed to eat the Bread of the Presence in the tabernacle. In the time of David, it was prophesied that David's house would be the lineage from which the Messiah would one day come.

In 1 Samuel 21, as David was fleeing for his life from Saul and his men, David was hungry and ran into the safe place of the priests. The only thing there to eat was the Bread of the Presence, so the priest gave it to David.

Nowhere else in Scripture had anyone outside of the priesthood eaten the Bread of the Presence. It was consecrated bread. This is another quiet prophetic moment that means so much when you see it, because from the line of David, Jesus would come.

And Yeshua says he is the Bread of Life.

John 6:35, translated from the Aramaic Bible into Plain English 2010, reads: "Yeshua said to them, 'I AM THE LIVING GOD, The Bread of Life; whoever comes to me shall not hunger, and whoever trusts in me shall never thirst.'"

"I am the living bread that came down from heaven. If anyone eats of this bread, he will live forever. And the bread that I will give for the life of the world is my flesh." (John 6:51 ESV)

In Luke 22:19, Jesus is having the Last Supper with the disciples. "And he took bread, and when he had given thanks, he broke it and gave it to them, saying, 'This is my body, which is given for you. Do this in remembrance of me.'"

As we ask for our daily bread, we continue to acknowledge the Giver along with our own need, and we also acknowledge His presence, which was given in the bodily form of Yeshua. We are to remember Him and think of Him on a daily basis as what was "given" to us. He said He was the bread from Heaven just like the manna, some of which was kept in the tabernacle in the Holy of Holies.

We can think of our Provider giving us what we need every day. We need Him present in our day-to-day, as He loves us in a deeper way and meaning, all the while providing as we come to Him. He gave His body and His blood for our atonement which is the payment for our sins so that we could be present with Him for eternity. "Give us this day our daily bread."

He desires our words and the power He placed in them for intimacy and communion. The depth of communion is rich in our receiving of the elements of bread and wine as blood and body, as well as our daily needs being met in body and in the presence of the Spirit.

His Body took every kind of curse and sin. His body represented in communion is our healing and deliverance. It is also in the communion of talking with Him, listening to Him, and spending time in His presence. He made the first move. It's up to us to respond.

Yeshua said to partake in communion often in remembrance of Him. Remembering Him like this keeps up our relationship and helps to keep us trusting in Who He is and all He has given for us in order to have this kind of relationship with Him and this kind of health, healing and wholeness because of what He did for us through His own body.

"And forgive us our trespasses as we forgive those who trespass against us"

Forgiveness is key to all relationships. In our imperfection, we are bound to be selfish at some point and hurt someone else just like they are likely to do that to us or someone else.

"For all have sinned and fall short of the glory of God." (Romans 3:23) When we recognize each other as the same in this regard, it helps remove judgment toward other people. We are broken and can't do everything we are supposed to. The only one who could fulfill the law perfectly was Yeshua.

We start out with expectations from our parents to be a certain way, do a certain thing, and accomplish what they say. When we don't, we either lie about it, try to take it or make it happen in unearned ways, or we become angry and rebel against them.

When the world says we should look a certain way or have something we don't, we believe the lie that we are inferior just like the lie Satan hissed to Eve. We often respond in broken ways if we aren't able to meet those expectations. We sin. Sometimes we have pains or an emptiness that we try to fill and Satan is quick to set up a temptation that is separate from God.

When we realize this, it is easier to forgive people because we are not sitting in a place of judgment, but in a place of empathy and understanding. "For all have sinned and fall short of the glory of God." (Romans 3:23)

Unforgiveness gets in the way of relationship not only with that person but also with YHVH.

I give a demonstration in one of my teachings using arrows. I pretend that the arrows were shot into me by placing them under my arms and holding some between my legs, and I try to walk and move. In order to keep them in place, my movement is restricted. Each arrow represents unforgiveness for someone or something that caused me pain that I was still carrying around.

Unforgiveness is like that. It restricts us and keeps us away from a close relationship with someone else. It gets in the way. It also takes up a place in our lives where YHVH is not.

As I demonstrated forgiveness, one at a time, I started to release the arrows in front of them. After removing them, I set them on something else as if it is Yeshua taking them. Then I am able to move freely. I take big strides, turn, and give hugs without out anything in the way.

Forgiving is freeing and opens us up. It also allows YHVH into those places that had been holding on to hurt so he can fill them, heal them, and make them well. Forgiving has been the most life-giving and liberating thing I have been able to do for myself.

Know the power of this.

This is the place of major restoration, power, grace, hope, life, and an eternal relationship when our own sins are forgiven through Yeshua.

I then have the people in my class pray and ask Yeshua to show them who they may have unforgiveness for. I did this in my own life and was amazed at who Yeshua showed me. I had forgotten about many of them but had still harbored unforgiveness anyway. As Yeshua reminded me of people in those months, I saw all sorts of look-a-likes of people I hadn't thought of for years.

One time, I saw a musician that I had not cared for simply because I thought he got attention for his music more so due to the incredible vocals of others rather than his own. I resented him for it. Resentment is a cousin of unforgiveness. It takes up space.

I was at an event specifically for healing and freeing. In my own self-assuredness, I thought I would be learning about it to teach others, but Yeshua had plans to heal *me*. At the start of the course, a film played, featuring this very musician I had resented. He spoke of his childhood abuse and said that only by Yeshua helping him to forgive was he able to move on.

Talk about YHVH giving me an ample lapful of conviction by His Spirit. YHVH wasn't condemning me, but He *was* convicting me... and I had asked for it.

When I let that go, I felt so much better. I was grateful YHVH loved me enough to show me that. Now I can walk in freedom from it, and I have that much more of His love and presence in my life instead.

One woman came back a week later after having attended that particular class that I taught on forgiveness. She said that she had a stack of 3x5 cards of people she was shown she hadn't forgiven.

She was shocked by it all, but the freedom she was feeling was powerful and wonderful. It is amazing what kinds of arrows we are carrying around in us.

Let it go. Release it. Give it to Yeshua.

The fullness of what Yahweh has *always* offered to us is forgiveness. He was forgiving before He came as Yeshua. The wages of sin is death, but YHVH provided a way through sacrifices made at the tabernacle for sins until the time was right for Yeshua. There was a payment in the life of an animal life without any kind of blemish.

My car was stolen a little over a year ago. It was found shortly later, and when I picked it up from the police station, it was filthy inside. I had to spend a fair amount of money to get it cleaned and get the smells out, not to mention paying the towing charge.

The person that stole it was caught and found guilty. I received a letter from the court system asking me to estimate the expenses that I had incurred with respect to the theft. That amount was to be awarded to me. A while later, I received another letter that named the individual. Next to his name was the word "Debtor."

Right away, I thought of the song of *The Lord's Prayer* where the lyrics say, "and forgive us our debts as we forgive our debtors." I knew I had to forgive him. If I signed the document, a "judgment" would follow him until it was paid. I couldn't ignore how Yeshua paid my own debt and that judgment no longer followed me.

The word "forbear" popped into my head.

When a word comes to mind that I had not processed anything to arrive at it, I pay attention to it and usually do a little more digging. Forbearance in Hebrew is the word *kaaphar*, which is the word used for atonement.

It is also used for the first time in describing the "Seat of Atonement" in the Holy of Holies. This is the gold covering the Ark of the Covenant. The priest that was allowed to go in would take the blood from the sacrifice and rub the blood onto the atonement seat with his finger.

I thought of Yeshua and how His own blood dripped from His fingers, atoning for our sin. He is called the Chief Priest. The connections YHVH makes are too many to ignore or dismiss. He helps us to believe by transforming them into a revelation or a picture for us to easily understand. He gave me a word and let me dig.

The other remarkable part was that this letter, with this great lesson for me, was delivered to me on the day of Yom Kippur, the Hebrew day for atonement.

Only YHVH could have put all of those details together to give me this picture of forgiveness.

He communicates to us 24/7. Open yourself up to learn from Him. He has an endless supply to give to you to grow your life and to live it more abundantly. Not all of it is easy, but all of it is for growth and for our benefit.

My son complains about the pain in his legs at times. They are growing pains. We need to understand that even in the spiritual, there are times that are growing pains, but it will grow us and make us stronger and mature us to be that much more whole and well in ourselves and for others.

"And lead us not into temptation, but deliver us from evil."

Yeshua speaks from the heart here. He includes this in the prayer of relationship with the Father so we are engaging our words with Him to not be separated from Him and we need His help. The first thing that happened to Yeshua after His baptism and start into ministry was that the Holy Spirit led him into the desert to be tempted. This was the will of YHVH, and He was the one leading so we could see how to withstand the tempter, Satan.

Yeshua endured forty days of fasting and temptations by Satan. He was offered power, riches, and even food to His starving body, but He refused to take anything given by Satan.

He was tested, and tests help us to become aware of what we know and what we need to know better. Yeshua's victory over Satan came through speaking words against the temptations. He spoke the Word spoken by Yahweh.

---

2 And when He had fasted forty days and forty nights, afterward He was hungry. 3 Now when the tempter came to Him, he said, "If You are the Son of God, command that these stones become bread." 4 But He answered and said, "It is written, 'Man shall not live by bread alone, but by every

word that proceeds from the mouth of God.'" (Matthew 4:2-4 NKJ)

One time, when Yeshua was tempted by Peter to use His power and avoid the cross, Yeshua replied, "Get behind Me, Satan." Not that Peter himself was Satan, but those thoughts and words were not of Yahweh. Satan used the words of a friend to tempt Him not to go forward. He was telling Satan to get out of His way.

The temptations of Satan are designed to thwart Yahweh's will and to keep us in bondage. Satan comes to rob, steal, and destroy not only what is ours but also what is Yahweh's.

Yahweh allowed this time of tempting early on so that Yeshua would have the strength to endure an even more tempting time coming up—one where obedience to the cross was the most important thing. He got a workout and a practice run.

We also got an example of the sufferings Yeshua instantly began to endure when He made His public display of obedience by doing the work set before Him.

Sometimes our greater hardships can be a time of strengthening, but they are still hard, just like working out our muscles. It isn't easy, and it involves effort on our part, but we do end up stronger afterward.

The new commitment to a life in Yeshua brings about an early round of temptations to attempt to draw us away from it. I sometimes wonder if it is our testing to strengthen us for the greater purposes Yahweh has planned for us need the dedication of faithfulness and obedience.

We quickly begin to learn the sacrifice it takes, and we become acquainted with His sufferings. Yeshua included this portion in the prayer to not be led into temptation, and to be delivered from evil.

By the grace and strength of His Holy Spirit in us, He can deliver us. Sometimes we are stronger after having said "no" to temptation. We become all the more committed until eventually, the temptation becomes so grotesque or completely forgotten about that it loses any strength or power against us. Yeshua spoke this part of the prayer from a tried and true place of empathy to maintain a right relationship with the Father.

Hebrews 14:5 says, "For we do not have a high priest who is unable to empathize with our weaknesses, but we have one who has been tempted in every way, just as we are--yet he did not sin."

A regular connection to Yahweh helps to keep us strong. With Alcoholics Anonymous, members can call a sponsor when feeling tempted to have a drink. The person called will help them out of it, often by identifying with the caller and caring for them. The ongoing meetings are a dependable source that maintains helpful relationships and accountability and support.

Yahweh is our call when we are weak, and sometimes Yahweh sends help without us asking for it. When Yeshua finished His time in the desert with Satan, angels were sent to strengthen Him: "Then the devil left him, and angels came and attended him." (Matthew 4:11)

Also, while in Gethsemane and in anguish about what He was about to do in way of crucifixion and taking on our sins, Yeshua asked that the cup be passed from Him. Yet Yeshua also prayed, "Not my will but Yours be done." Immediately after, in John 22:43, it reads, "And there appeared to him an angel from heaven, strengthening him."

Yahweh will give you strength as you live in obedience to Him, and He will deliver you. Understanding this kind of relationship and knowing how important your words and prayers are to Him brings comfort, strength, grace, peace, and hope.

Some churches teach the Lord's Prayer with an additional portion: **"For thine is the kingdom and the power and the glory, forever and ever. Amen."** This portion was added 100 years after Christ in a response of giving him honor above all else.

"Through whom we have gained access by faith into this grace in which we now stand. And we rejoice in the hope of the glory of God." (Romans 5:2)

We are provided the way to commune, communicate, and talk to Yahweh through prayer. When we know, see, and believe everything that has been given to us, we can come to Him fully. His Power is released into our lives as we release our lives to Him. It is a surrender prayer.

These verses point us into a fullness of life in our ability to come to Yahweh confidently in our relationship made and provided by Him:

"So do not throw away your confidence; it will be richly rewarded." (Hebrews 10:35)

"For Christ also suffered once for sins, the righteous for the unrighteous, that he might bring us to God, being put to death in the flesh but made alive in spirit." (1 Peter 3:18)

"Dear friends, if our hearts do not condemn us, we have confidence before God." (1 John 3:21)

"And this is the confidence that we have toward him, that if we ask anything according to his will he hears us. And if we know that he hears us in whatever we ask, we know that we have the requests that we have asked of him.." (1 John 5:14-15)

"And the peace of God, which surpasses all understanding, will guard your hearts and your minds in Christ Jesus. And the peace of God, which surpasses all understanding, will guard your hearts and your minds in Christ Jesus(Philippians 4:6-7)

He's there for us.

He wants us to tell Him what we want or need and to be thankful for what He has given. When we remember what He has done, it is easier to believe He will continue to do for us.

Philippians 4:6 says to "present" our requests. I have learned to envision myself handing them to Yahweh. It helps me to let go of them when I do that. I even go so far as to physically hold out my hands in the gesture. When I do that, my I feel a releasing of my cares and concerns.

He says to "cast our cares on Him" because He cares for us. He wants us to live free and enjoy the life He has given us and not worry. He wants to give us that peace that we can't even put into words. His peace is another example of His presence and our willingness to be open to receive Him. Again, it is an example of intimacy.

"Then Jesus said, 'Come to me, all of you who are weary and carry heavy burdens, and I will give you rest.'" (Matthew 11:28)

"I will refresh the weary and satisfy the faint." (Jeremiah 31:25)

This is a time for more prayer in areas of your life where you may not have prayed. Start by finding a place and time where you can bring your whole self before Him.

Think on your close relationship of being both family and friend with Him.

Think about who He is and all that He has for you.

Begin to find peace and rest in His presence, and let Him restore and refill you. If you aren't noticing it, ask Him to let you really notice it. There is no detail too little to ask for.

Begin to spend time forgiving people who have hurt or wronged you. Pray good for their lives. Ask Yahweh to remind you of people you may have not forgiven, even if you have forgotten about them, even those whom you may hold resentment toward. The release and healing is so freeing to open your life and prayer life up that much more.

"The thief cometh not, but that he may steal, and kill, and destroy: I came that they may have life, and may have it abundantly." (John 10:10 ASV)

"When you forgive this man, I forgive him, too. And when I forgive whatever needs to be forgiven, I do so with Christ's authority for your benefit, 11 so that Satan will not outsmart us. For we are familiar with his evil schemes." (1 Corinthians 2:10-11 NLT)

Unforgiveness often coats itself with hate, anger, or pride. Don't let Satan get a foothold into your life through unforgiveness.

You have been learning to see yourself as Yahweh sees you. Yeshua gives us more clues of what the enemy does and what He/Yeshua does instead. Let's know the difference and live a life of abundance.

Learning and living in a new life of righteousness—Yeshua's righteousness—there are many good things and help along the way. James 5:16 says, "Therefore confess your sins to each other and pray for each other so that you may be healed. The prayer of a righteous person is powerful and effective."

We see Yahweh's continued use of relationships in this verse for good.

Has someone ever shared their past sins and then the new change that happened in their life, and it blessed you to know that Yeshua helped them overcome it? While we are in the midst of those sins, it is sometimes difficult to overcome them alone. Consider asking for prayer from someone you trust who walks closely with Yeshua.

This is an excerpt from Matthew Henry's commentary on this verse on BibleHub.com.

To acknowledge our faults to each other, will tend greatly to peace and brotherly love. And when a righteous person, a true believer, justified in Christ, and by his grace walking before Yahweh in holy obedience, presents an effectual fervent prayer, wrought in his heart by the power of the Holy Spirit, raising holy affections and believing expectations and so leading earnestly to plead the promises of Yahweh at his mercy-seat, it avails much. The power of prayer is proved from the history of Elijah. In prayer we must not look to the merit of man, but to the grace of Yahweh. This instance of the power of prayer, encourages every Christian to be earnest in prayer. God never says to any of the seed of Jacob, Seek my face in vain. Where there may not be so much of miracle in God's answering our prayers, yet there may be as much of grace.

Some translate the word "inspired" as the Spirit of God breathing into men the breath of spiritual life.Those living spiritually inspired are and being quickened by Him., inspired by Him. Prayer is so important to the spiritual life that prayer can be thought of as the life-breath of the spiritual man.

"Rejoice always, 17 pray without ceasing, 18 give thanks in all circumstances; for this is the will of God in Christ Jesus for you. 19 Do not quench the Spirit. 20 Do not despise prophecies, 21 but test everything; hold fast what is good. 22 Abstain from every form of evil. (1 Thessalonians 5:16-22)

"And pray in the Spirit on all occasions with all kinds of prayers and requests. With this in mind, be alert and always keep on praying for all the Lord's people." (Ephesians 6:18)

We have a helper in praying in the Spirit, and we also have helpers in our relationships as we pray for the Creator's people and they in turn pray for us. We back each other up, and the Creator/Yahweh backs us up by His Spirit.

"In the same way, the Spirit helps us in our weakness. We do not know what we ought to pray for, but the Spirit himself intercedes for us through wordless groans. And he who searches our hearts knows the mind of the Spirit, because the Spirit intercedes for God's people in accordance with the will of God." (Romans 8:26-27)

And we also see in verse 34: "Who then is the one who condemns? No one. Christ Yeshua who died—more than that, who was raised to life—is at the right hand of God and is also interceding for us." (Romans 8:34)

Grab a hold of this: Praying in the Spirit is a powerful intercession, and it is why Ephesians 6:18 says to pray in the Spirit in all occasions.

We have been given the *Ruah*, the breath/spirit, and our prayers are received as a fragrance to Him filled with His Spirit. The gift of tongues is a powerful gift of prayer and one worth asking for. It is the language of the Holy Spirit upon your breath.

In our moments of trailing thoughts or imperfect prayers, Yeshua is interceding on our behalf in a full measure into righteousness, perfect in every way.

In John 17:6-26, Yeshua prays for his disciples and for us. It is worth stopping for a moment and opening your Bible to read this for yourself.

Take it to heart, and let His words to the Father bless you in a deep and intimate way as He prays for you. Underline it or highlight it. You are loved!

CHAPTER ELEVEN
PRAYING FOR OTHERS

A CALL FOR WARRIORS

Intercessory prayer is another way of saying you are praying for someone else. It's that simple. Sometimes you hear the word intercessor or prayer warrior, that's the person who is praying for someone else or something else.

Additionally, the phrase "standing in the gap" means the intercessor is the connecting part between acknowledging Yahweh and the person you are praying for, or a situation you are praying about.

This phrase comes from Ezekiel 22:30 NLT: " I looked for someone who might rebuild the wall of righteousness that guards the land. I searched for someone to stand in the gap in the wall so I wouldn't have to destroy the land, but I found no one."

We know Yahweh loves us and wants us to talk to Him.

There is more.

He calls us to pray not only for ourselves and to converse with Him but also to lift others in prayer before Him. This is where our relationships, our placement in life and in the lives of others, and our individual interests, compassions, and passions come into great purpose.

There is only one you. Only you know the people you know, and only you have the relationships that you have. Only you have been given an interest and passion in certain areas based on your own circumstances, interests, places you've lived, and point of view. These are all areas God can use for great purposes through you and you alone.

~

Over twenty years ago, I heard about a young mom whose baby girl had an emergency situation and needed to be taken by an ambulance. She shared how she had always prayed for ambulances whenever she saw them. She would pray for the people needing them, the people that were giving medical care, and for the driver.

Then she found herself in an ambulance with her little girl and she thought how surely there were others praying for them as they traveled to the hospital. It gave her comfort.

This story moved me. I had never thought to do this, and it changed me. I became an avid prayer person this way. I prayed for the ambulances as I thought of her story. I even began praying for people in the hospitals as I drove past them.

I especially prayed for children I saw outside or when I drove by schools. Yahweh had given me a heart for children. This was part of the way I was made.

My mom would pray whenever she saw an airplane overhead. We lived near a major airport and the planes are frequent. She prayed for the passengers, thinking of their business or family visits, vacations, or maybe a need to see someone who was sick or attend a funeral. She also prayed for the pilots and flight attendants. She thought and prayed for a lot of situations.

I have heard some pretty great stories of people praying for others or changing lives while they flew next to someone on an airplane. Sometimes I wonder if God also partnered with someone on the ground through their prayers.

We didn't know whom we were praying for, but we prayed nonetheless. Some people pray for their government because they are politically minded. Some think and pray for soldiers, some for truck drivers, some for teachers, and some when they pass by nursing homes or for the land, water, and against spiritual strongholds.

One day, a woman walked along the sidewalk in front of my parents' house. My dad was outside. His house was for sale, and the "For Sale" sign was up. The woman spoke to him and told him that she always prays for the houses she sees that are for sale. She prays for a sale, for blessed buyers and blessed sellers, and that Yahweh would make good homes for them both. She said she would be praying for his.

There are endless ways to pray and endless things to pray about. I have learned that when someone comes to mind, I will pray for them. It is a lot more fun to tell them I was praying for them than to say I was thinking of them.

Sometimes I don't see that person but later hear that they had been going through something where prayers were needed. God loves to partner with us when He is moving. When we act on his urging, it helps build our faith.

God showed me a couple of ways how He was partnering with me in what He had planned and was doing. I didn't know them at the time, so I just prayed.

I mentioned earlier that I have a tender heart toward children. While I was in the car one morning driving to work, I saw a little boy standing outside by the street corner. He was dressed like one of the characters from *The Blues Brothers*.

He was a plump little boy and wore a hat and sunglasses, and he was holding a saxophone. His mom was taking his picture by the street sign.

I began praying for him, and my prayers took off in the Spirit. It was so strong as I prayed and I wondered why I cared so much in the Spirit about this little boy whom I had never met. Then I continued driving to work.

When my daughter was eighteen years old, she started dating a guy she met from the swim team at her high school. He wasn't a Christian, and she made it clear to him that church was important to her, and so was her faith. She told him that if he wanted any part of her life, he would have to come to church with her. He agreed and came to sit with her each week.

One Sunday, a particular worship song really moved him. He realized he wanted to have a life in Christ and became a follower of Yeshua. The song playing that moved him to this decision was *Lord, Reign In Me*. It meant so much to him that he later got a tattoo on his arm with a cross and "Reign In Me" written on it.

One day, my daughter and this boyfriend were talking about when they were little. He shared how he had been really short and chubby like our daughter had been in middle school. It was funny because he was now 6' 4" and very thin.

She went and got pictures of herself, and he went home to get his. We looked through the stack and found a photo of him dressed as a Blues Brother with a saxophone standing by the street sign.

He was the little boy I'd seen years earlier! Yeshua cared so much for him that he had me partner in prayer for him. Not only did Yahweh love him, but He showed His love for me by showing His power and love by letting me see the grown boy and the evidence through that picture. He has given me this story and strengthened my faith in prayer.

The young man and my daughter later ended their relationship, but he continued to come to the church and often sat with our family. He frequently played his saxophone with the worship/music team at church services and for special programs.

Later, he gave his testimony in front of the church congregation of how he came to Yeshua through the music of that church and because of the insistence of a girl he was dating. His only access to her was if he came to church.

Later, he married a friend of our daughter's who attended that church, too. Yahweh is good. He has a plan, and He invites us to participate in what He is doing through our beautiful ability to pray with the breath He has given us. Our lives matter, and He gives purpose to our breath by His Spirit.

Another time much later, I was going through some important changes in my life. I felt Yahweh tell me to go to Pine Ridge in South Dakota to pray. This was God's biggest request of me regarding prayer to date, but I packed up my car, never having traveled anywhere on my own like that, and started driving.

A friend of mine arranged a meeting for me to meet a couple of people there. Yahweh told me to pray for them and to hold my arms out over them. I was so afraid! I barely held my arms out. They looked like stubby chicken wings. But I prayed.

Soon after, through miraculously coming across one of the men a couple more times in another state, I ended up writing his story. It is called, *A Warrior's Circle of Yesterday, Today and Tomorrow*, and it is helping many people.

If I hadn't gone to Pine Ridge, I would not have met him and written the book. That book was a three-year journey of many ups and many downs in the process of writing it. It has brought my relationship with Yahweh to a level I would have never had, if I had not obeyed Him.

I have peace knowing I walked according to His will. It was also a time to gain bravery. Now when I pray for people, my arms reach out like eagle wings instead of chicken wings.

Yahweh does so much when we open our lives every day to Him. When we really walk with Him and breathe Him in and know how much He loves us, He's powerfully active. He puts us in the places that He desires for a purpose... *His* purpose. He gives us a will to choose. That is part of the beauty of the freedom when we choose Him.

I mentioned how cold Minnesota is. I don't like the cold. I love heat and humidity, and I often wondered why Yahweh had me living in Minnesota.

Awhile back, I was in Florida visiting my parents. I was doing my usual complaining, wondering why on earth Yahweh would have me live in Minnesota. I believed I was made for Florida as I sat in the warm sun.

A friend of my Mom's had been listening to me, and he stood up, towering over me, and looked down at me lying there. He said, "You aren't in Minnesota for you. You're in Minnesota for God."

Wow. He silenced me in a flash. Like lightning. I remember my Mom's mouth dropping open along with mine. I will not soon forget these strong, powerful words.

So here I sit, typing during a blizzard and hearing thunder at the same time. But I'm here for Him, and He uses my purpose, my place, my relationships, and my interests to know Him more and to bless others through my own life and God-given breath.

Where are you? You have much to do there. You have been created for more.

When Yahweh decides to reveal why He had you pray, it builds your faith. Your praying does so much to build your own faith when you act in obedience and He later shows you why you were moved to pray.

A beautiful thing happened at this point of writing this book. I had wrapped up my writing for the day and thought of a friend of mine. I decided to pray for her, and I let her know that I had done so.

She responded with gratitude and thanked me as a friend, as a sister in faith, and teacher. She said that what I had taught her about praying for others when they come to mind had given her a joy and peace like none other. She thanked me for showing her that.

Not only was she blessed by my prayers, but the return was exactly what I needed. Her words encouraged me at this exact time of writing on this exact subject. It affirmed my current work.

At times, in all honesty, when you are in the midst of a project you feel you are doing out of obedience to Yahweh, you sometimes wonder if it was worth it. In spite of the amount of effort and no knowledge of any good coming of it, was it really for Him after all?

Yahweh blessed me through her words. I had not known if she had ever grasped that part of what I had taught on prayer before. Her words blessed me with a new certainty in the writing and the time commitment that it has taken in research, prayer, and effort in placing these words together.

Yahweh loves to weave within our lives and create and prove His undeniable presence amidst our lives in precise, perfected timing.

This woman whom I had felt led to pray for was only three weeks from passing away at the time. Those were the last words I ever heard from her. I had known she was ill, but I had no idea how far the cancer had progressed.

I went to see her a few days before she died. She was unable to respond or communicate, but I prayed love and gratitude for her life. She had shared encouraging words with so many. What she had given to me without speaking of her own troubles was an incredible, unselfish, generosity.

Intercession, praying for others, is a ministry of divine appointment. "For if you remain silent at this time, relief and deliverance for the Jews will arise from another place, but you and your father's family will perish. And who knows but that you have come to royal position for such a time as this?" (Esther 4:14)

Esther is a book about intercession.

Even in silence there could be death.

Speaking, in Esther's case, was the only hope for life for her and her family.

Through a series of miraculous favor, Esther was given the position of Queen. All along the way, her cousin Mordecai looked out for her and guided her. She had been an orphan, and Mordecai cared for her and brought her up.

When she became Queen, he sat at the gates of the Kingdom, observing and watching over all that was happening to Esther. He was keeping watch. They were Jews, and at that time, they were thought of as lowly. The king was not aware of Esther's blood line before they married.

One day, Mordecai overheard the plans of the king's evil right-hand man, named Haman. The king had already proclaimed and signed into law that which Haman had wanted... the killing of all of the Jews.

Mordecai pled with Esther to help save their people. Only she had access to the king. Esther then told Mordecai to tell all of the people to fast for three days while she prayed and prepared for what she must do. She was to approach the king without having been invited to do so. This could be reason alone for death in those times.

As Mordecai interceded for the people in asking Esther for her help, Esther in turn asked for the interceding of the people to help her by prayer and fasting.

Mordecai insists that Yahweh's plan would take place. He would keep His people safe and would not let them come to complete destruction.

But if Esther did not step in, she herself would have lost her own life in the way of disobedience and not trusting God. She would lose the testimony of His salvation and greatness and therefore would have no heritage of faith to pass on to her children and family.

As Esther listened to Mordecai regarding this she said, Go, gather all the Jews to be found in Susa, and hold a fast on my behalf, and do not eat or drink for three days, night or day. I and my young women will also fast as you do. Then I will go to the king, though it is against the law, and if I perish, I perish. (Esther 4:16 ESV)

Esther showed that she cared for her people by believing and walking in faith. Doing what was right in her faith and spirit was more important than a physical death.

> On the third day Esther put on her royal robes and stood in the inner court of the palace, in front of the king's hall. The king was sitting on his royal throne in the hall, facing the entrance. When he saw Queen Esther standing in the court, he was pleased with her and held out to her the gold scepter that was in his hand. So Esther approached and touched the tip of the scepter. (Esther 5:1-2)

We have seen verses saying that because of what Yeshua did for us, we can now come boldly and confidently before Him. Here's another:

> "I delight greatly in Yahweh; my soul rejoices in my God. For he has clothed me with garments of salvation and arrayed me in a robe of righteousness, as a bridegroom adorns his head like a priest, and as a bride adorns herself with her jewels." (Isaiah 61:10)

Likewise, Esther used her position as bride and adorned herself before coming to the throne. Christ's intercession for us becomes the garments of salvation and a robe of righteousness.

> Then Queen Esther answered, "If I have found favor with you, O king, and if it pleases your majesty, grant me my life—this is my petition. And spare my people—this is my request. For I and my people have been sold for destruction and slaughter and

annihilation. If we had merely been sold as male and female slaves, I would have kept quiet, because no such distress would justify disturbing the king. (Esther 7:3-4)

She would not have bothered the king with something her people could have endured and suffered through. This travesty would be unbearable, so she asked for mercy.

My grandmother prayed for the generations to come and told us about the generations before her. It is known among all of the great-grandchildren and the great-great grand children that our great-great grandmother prayed for her children, her children's children, their children after them, and so on.

The knowledge of her words of faith and prayers that carried through generations lingers in our hearts and minds as we, too, have learned to pray that way. She spoke it out. We know other relatives prayed and believed and showed actions of faith. Because her words were spoken to us about these prayers, it strengthened our connection to the importance of the generations and our relationship spiritually with God.

In the Gospel of Mark, Yeshua goes before God the Father prior to His crucifixion. He brought Peter, James, and John with Him to stand watch as His intercessors as He was about to intercede for us.

---

33 He took Peter, James and John along with him, and he began to be deeply distressed and troubled. 34 "My soul is overwhelmed with sorrow to the point of death," he said to them. "Stay here and keep watch."

35 Going a little farther, he fell to the ground and prayed that if possible the hour might pass from him. 36 "Abba,

Father," he said, "everything is possible for you. Take this cup from me. Yet not what I will, but what you will." (Mark 14:33-35)

Yeshua fell to the ground before the Creator in prayer and anguish for what was to come. He prayed His requests and used His position of Son as He called God, "Abba, Father."

But He held the Creator in authority and showed that He would always follow His will.

Yeshua saw that Peter, James, and John had fallen asleep again. This can serve as a metaphor of people who believe in Yeshua but fall asleep in the efforts of prayer and watching out for others.

We stop paying attention or noticing. We are easily tempted by our own desires and distractions even though remaining prayerful and watchful has great importance to keep us from temptation.

"Then he returned to his disciples and found them sleeping. 'Simon,' he said to Peter, 'are you asleep? Could you not keep watch for one hour? 38 Watch and pray so that you will not fall into temptation. The spirit is willing, but the body is weak.'" (Mark 14:37-38)

Our strength comes from a relationship with Yahweh. Often we want that relationship, but we don't do a good job at developing it, including asking for His help.

We need to pray.

These are characteristics of intercessors. We can see them in both Esther's and Jesus' example:

- Selflessness and self discipline
- Obedience

- Persistence and determination
- Patience
- Faith
- Spirit placed burden
- Love for others
- Willing to give up one's self for Yahweh's will/Sacrifice

Intercession sometimes involves fasting. In addition to the Book of Esther, some examples of that are found in Deuteronomy 9, Ezra 10, Daniel 9, Joel 2, Jonah 3, and Matthew 4.

As a group of believers join together, there is strength with one another in Him. Again, this is part of our relationships.

"I have posted watchmen on your walls, O Jerusalem; they will never be silent day or night. You who call on the Yahweh, give yourselves no rest, 7 and give him no rest till he establishes Jerusalem and makes her the praise of the earth." (Isaiah 62:6-7)

When He prayed in Gethsemane, Yeshua didn't call just one disciple to "watch" but three. He drew upon their close relationship with Him and expected them to be strong together.

As people who have been asked to pray, you are appointed into a role you were called to do. If you have ever thought of someone and shortly later saw them or heard something about them, you have been nudged by His Spirit. Some call it intuition, but it is placed upon you by your Creator.

It is part of His power and your purpose with great love.

To those that have prayed for others: You are the ones carrying the beggars, blind, and lame, for you hear Him and know Him and follow

His ways. The Lord has given you eyes to see and ears to hear. This call is for a purpose far greater than you can know.

If you haven't prayed in this way for others, follow those promptings when you get them. It is the beginning of learning how to walk by His Spirit. Believe that the prayers open wide His door of blessings to come. His Kingdom waits for the requests of its people.

∼

It used to be hard for me to step in and pray. Years ago, I was at a conference, and the speaker sat on a stool on the stage. There were around 700 people present. I strongly sensed YHVH telling me to go up and place a hand on him and speak a short prayer over him. YHVH told me what I was to say. It was only three sentences long.

I started to panic and didn't want to do it. I questioned if YHVH really wanted me to do that. It seemed ridiculous, not to mention incredibly embarrassing to walk up out of all of those people and go on stage and pray for him.

A man sitting in front of me had been rocking side-to-side for more than ten minutes. It irritated me, and I wished for a while that he would stop, but he hadn't.

As I thought of this absurd request to go up and pray, I said to YHVH in my mind, "Okay, YHVH, if that is really You, make that man stop."

I had not even sounded the "p" out in my mind for "stop," and he stopped rocking.

My heart pounded in my chest, and I *knew* I had to go forward. Once again, in a panic of knowing His instruction, I told YHVH my part of the conditions. I can be dangerously bold sometimes, and He could have chosen not to help, but by His grace and His desire for me to act, He acted.

I told Him, "*You* are going to have to tell me when to go do it."

The speaker went into a prayer time where we all prayed quietly to ourselves. Then he started singing the song, *Arise, My Child*.

It was soft and sweet and gentle. I knew that was my cue.

I got up. I kept my head down the whole way up, so embarrassed and hoping no one knew me. I didn't know if he had guards or bouncers who would grab me and pull me away or if he would tell me to get down from the stage or get upset with me approaching.

I walked up the stairs, placed my hand on him and said the words God had given me to share. He looked up at me with the kindest and warmest smile.

I quickly turned away after I said it, and again and again, I heard him say, "Thank you, Jesus. Thank you, Jesus."

Whatever it was, it was between him and Jesus/Yeshua. I never found out why or what, but I knew Yeshua did something for him in that moment. I couldn't wait to get out of there. I was still embarrassed, but my desire to do as Yahweh asked overcame my desire to not obey.

I shared this experience with some women I was teaching, and another woman shared a time when she was asked by YHVH to do something weird. She was led to go to a person's feet and pray over them. She did it.

After the prayer time broke up, the woman next to her said to her that she had felt that same nudge but didn't do it. It is an example that YHVH's desires will take place, but we have the choice to partner with Him or not.

Had either one of us not been in regular relationship with YHVH in prayer, it would have been easy to not have acted. Many of us wish that we would do such a thing, with the Spirit being willing, but our flesh is weak. My weakness was still prominent as I put conditions up for YHVH to answer in order to make me feel confident enough to do it.

Our flesh *is* weak. We need His help. He helps us to believe.

Not everyone YHVH calls you to pray for knows Him. YHVH will prompt us to pray for people who don't know Him or for people who are in the midst of wicked lives. He welcomes the hands of the wicked to be made clean. It is His heart.

Don't let a criticism of their life keep you from being open to those nudges. Keeping yourself from judging or being critical opens you up to the fullness of love and serving that Yeshua intended.

It is why the lifestyle of forgiveness is so important. Forgiveness is a humbling of yourself. When you are humbled, you are compassionate to the struggles of others. The person you are praying for may not have ever had a prayer lifted on their behalf before.

CHAPTER TWELVE
A JOURNEY'S PRAYERS

We have a strong heart for our friends and family. We have something invested in them. Prayers for friends and family can reach places only a close relationship can know. These relationships can also motivate us to be more devoted in those prayers and to go to greater lengths.

A beautiful example of friendship in bringing a friend before the Lord for healing is found in Luke 5:17-26. Some people knew that Yeshua was near and teaching. They brought a paralytic man to Him to be healed. The room was packed with people, and there was no way to get to Yeshua, so they climbed up onto the building with the paralyzed man on his mat.

They began to remove the tiles from the roof until they had created an opening big enough to lower their friend right in front of Yeshua. They went to great lengths and did not give up. They persisted until their friend was at the very feet of Yeshua/Jesus.

This is what it is like when we pray for our friends. We make intentional effort and place our might behind those prayers as we lift our friends or family and carry them and their needs to Yeshua. We persist and will not let anything stand in the way.

It says in verse 20: "When Yeshua saw *their* faith, he said, 'Friend, your sins are forgiven.'" (emphasis added)

Yeshua wasn't speaking of the faith of the man on the mat; he spoke of "their" faith, meaning that of his friends who had helped him. The relationship of these friends mattered, and so did their faith.

∽

Our relationships and our place within this world matter. This was the time and place, as He was speaking to religious leaders and teachers, to show them His authority over sin. Not only were the friends in the right place and time for their paralytic friend, but He used their faith and efforts as an example and teaching for others.

Our place and relationships are always filled with Yahweh's purpose if we stop and take notice. The joy of recognizing that value is fulfilling. Yeshua taught on his authority over sin and also showed His power in telling the man to stand up and walk. Yeshua's spoken word freed him from sin and healed him and testified to those who listened.

As Yeshua showed his forgiveness of sin, he left this place and went on and called Levi to be His follower. Levi was a tax collector and known sinner for his greed and unfair practices. As Yeshua called him to be a follower, He again showed His authority over sin and His forgiveness and the freedom for Levi to turn from sin into a new life.

He showed grace.

Levi called in his "friends"—fellow tax collectors—to eat with Yeshua. It demonstrates the ripple effect of how our friendships can impact others to know Yeshua, too. Levi's sinful past would serve a purpose to bring others to the company and presence of Yeshua so they could know him, too.

And when they came near to Jericho, a certain blind man was sitting on the side of the road and begging. 36 And he heard the sound of the crowd that passed by and he was asking, "Who is this?" 37 They were saying to him, "Yeshua the Nazarene passes by." 38 And he cried out and he said, "Yeshua, Son of

David, have mercy on me!" And those who were going in front of Yeshua were rebuking him that he should be quiet, but he was crying out even more, "Son of David, have mercy on me!" 40 And Yeshua stood still, and he commanded to bring him to him, and when he came near to him, he asked him, 41 And he said to him, "What do you want me to do for you?" But he said, "My Lord, that I may see." 42 And Yeshua said to him, "See; your faith has saved you." 43 And immediately he saw, and he was coming after him and he was praising God, and all the people who saw were giving glory to God.(Luke 18:35-42 Aramaic in Plain English)

Notice here a few things. The blind man was in the right place at the right time for this event. He didn't even "see" it coming, yet it came. He was in need, and Yeshua was there. He knew or had heard of healings by Yeshua and so he shouted out to Him.

This time, we see people trying to get in the way of what Yeshua could do. Not only were they unwilling intercessors but they also felt like these low and needy people weren't good enough to be noticed by Yeshua, so they told the blind man to get out of the way. The man persisted and did not allow them to shame him.

This is where I love seeing Yeshua make them participate with Him in spite of their initial unwillingness. It says in verse 40 that, "Yeshua stopped and ordered the man to be brought to him."

This blesses me. He ordered the ones who tried to interfere, who were closest to the blind man, who had been rebuking him, to help him.

Sometimes we need to stop assuming that someone is too low or unworthy. Take a moment and think if there is anyone you know whom you have ridiculed in your own mind or heart to be beyond worth interceding for.

Yeshua called the blind man to *speak* out loud what he wanted. When the blind man did, Yeshua also affirmed the man's faith and then healed him because of it. Many others heard and witnessed this exchange, and praise burst out among them.

∼

The example of the Centurion in Matthew 8:5-10 is that of an intercessor who brought his servant's needs to Jesus. The servant was someone that worked for the Centurion. Think too, of your workplace. There are people there who need Yeshua and may have terrible suffering.

Your life with Jesus puts you in a place of relationship with Him, and because of where you work, you are able to know your employees' or co-workers' needs. You're there for more than a paycheck.

---

5 When Yeshua had entered Capernaum, a centurion came to him, asking for help. 6 "Lord," he said, "my servant lies at home paralyzed and in terrible suffering." 7 Yeshua said to him, "I will go and heal him." 8 The centurion replied, "Lord, I do not deserve to have you come under my roof. But just say the word, and my servant will be healed. 9 For I myself am a man under authority, with soldiers under me. I tell this one, 'Go,' and he goes; and that one, 'Come,' and he comes. I say to my servant, 'Do this,' and he does it." 10 When Yeshua heard this, he was astonished and said to those following him, "I tell you the truth, I have not found anyone in Israel with such great faith." (Matthew 8:5-10)

The Centurion's faith was in Yeshua's authority. It was also in the knowledge of the power of a spoken command by one who is in authority.

Yeshua says to us in Luke 10:19: "Behold, I have given you

authority to tread on serpents and scorpions, and over all the power of the enemy, and nothing shall hurt you."

Use your authority!

> As Jesus went on from there, two blind men followed him, calling out, "Have mercy on us, Son of David!" 28 When he had gone indoors, the blind men came to him, and he asked them, "Do you believe that I am able to do this?" Yes, Lord," they replied. 29 Then he touched their eyes and said, "According to your faith will it be done to you." (Matthew 9:27-29)

Yeshua had them speak out their faith by asking them if they believe He is able. Words are powerful, which is why He has us profess with our mouths.

It is the application of our breath to our faith in talking to Him in relationship.

These two blind men had a friendship and a common need. Yeshua promises that the prayers and requests of more than one are highly regarded.

> "Again, I tell you that if two of you on earth agree about anything you ask for, it will be done for you by my Father in heaven. 20 For where two or three come together in my name, there am I with them." (Matthew 18:19-20)

This verse is also the basis behind what is called prayer ministry. When gatherings take prayer needs and people pray together, they are held strongly in faith, and He is there. Prayer ministry is also offered as prayer ministers meet with individuals, and together they pray over needs and desires with Yahweh in their midst.

He is calling us to relationship in this verse. He is all about relationship. It allows a witness to see the answers to the prayer, affirming the other and strengthening the validity of the testimony. It also doubles or triples the blessing as others who witness His answers are strengthened in faith.

In order to pray *with* another, those prayers are spoken.

Praying for your children is an area I feel strongly about. My children span a range of ages. I prayed for my children and continue to do so in their adulthood.

Not everything in their lives happened the way I thought it would or how I wanted it to, but YHVH answers prayers in different ways from how we thought, and His ways are always best. His ways are not our ways.

Even though I pray, my children are not immune to hardship and temptations. The world pulls strongly upon our kids, away from Yahweh. I walked that myself in my early twenties. It is especially true at that time as we are stepping out in independence. During our independence we have to find our own faith for ourselves, and it is an independent decision.

While I searched in ways that didn't lead to fulfillment, my parents and church and elders prayed for me, and I did eventually find the One who fulfilled me. Their prayers carried great purpose for my life, and I am doing more in living for Yahweh than ever before.

I've turned a half-century old and have never served Him more. I've suffered losses, but my relationship with Him has grown. It hasn't always been an easy relationship with YHVH, but He is Holy and uses all things for my benefit, even if I don't like it.

Never give up on praying for your children or the children of others. Don't think that Yahweh hasn't heard you. He gives us a will, and by that will He allows us to find Him for ourselves. The relationship He wants with us is personal. We can't forget that with our children.

Ultimately, it's up to God how He reveals Himself to them, and it will be up to them if they choose to come into relationship with Him, just like it was up to you when you decided to come into a relationship with Yahweh/the Creator.

You can't force another to do your will. Nor will this book force anyone into a relationship with their Creator. It is only by His Spirit that we are moved or begin to recognize our yearning for His presence. That's when it's the right time to say, "I want to know You, too."

I found some great areas to pray about for children in a book written by Stormie Omartian called *The Power of a Praying Parent*. I put together a list that stood out to me.

The first is to pray that the child would know the fullness of God's love. That's everything to me and at the top of my list.

Other suggestions included:

- Praying in their room, over their bed, in their closets and over and through your home
- Praying for their protection
- Wisdom and desire to follow God's best path
- Sensitive to His Spirit
- For their mates
- Identifying their gifts
- Filled with the joy of the Lord
- Against family inheritance of sin patterns or generational things
- Walk in repentance
- Grow in Faith

These are some suggestions that you may or may not have thought of, and you probably have your own wonderful thoughts on them.

In knowing who to pray for, this passage sums it up well for me:

> I urge, then, first of all, that requests, prayers, intercession and thanksgiving be made for *everyone*— 2 for kings and all those in authority, that we may live peaceful and quiet lives in all godliness and holiness. 3 This is good, and pleases God our Savior, 4 who wants all men to be saved and to come to a knowledge of the truth. (1 Timothy 2:1-4)

This is your pep talk. You are wonderfully created. You carry the essence of Yahweh/the Creator in the breath He breathed into your life, and you can receive of the breath of His Spirit. You are mostly made up of the miraculous essence of water that even Heaven itself has it in its name.

You are given the gift of words to be in a relationship with Him, communicating to commune. You get to talk to the Creator as your Daddy and Friend because of Yeshua's death and resurrection. And in those words His power through prayer opens you to the place of His presence—right into His chambers. You are invited.

We briefly looked at a key area in Esther. I'd like to share with you a portion of Beth Moore's Bible study on Esther. She writes:

> "How often does our own King hold out the scepter of His approval and though we inch forward in timid approach we choose not to reach out and touch it? Oh, that we'd receive such royal invitation even when our hearts pound within us until our ears ring! Who knows what a mighty deliverance is at hand?" (Esther; It's Tough Being a Woman: Beth Moore Lifeway Press; Nov 17, 2008)

"I am the Root and Offspring of David, and the bright Morning Star." The Spirit and the bride say, "Come!" (Revelation 22:16b-17a)

Your invitation into your royal position and family is made. Step up and reach out. This is your time, your purpose, and your position. Use your life for purposes that are eternal. You are made for this.

I like this quote by C.S. Lewis: "You don't have a soul; you are a soul. You have a body." Let's put the eternal in the here-and-now as we live in these bodies for such a time as this.

There is so much about prayer in the Bible. To spend a little bit exploring it in this book is like eating only one appetizer after a day of work in the fields. Our lives are deeply rich, complicated, intertwined, and full. Yahweh is there for all of it and there are so many examples of prayer in the Word as you read about the lives and living of people just like us.

You won't get full on the little bit I have shared, but I hope it will inspire an appetite for you to discover how much more is out there. Prayer is delicious and filling and satisfying in every need or desire you could possibly have. Look to the examples in the Bible as people called upon Yahweh as well as the prayers for you from your Brothers and Sisters in Christ. There are as many prayers as there are thoughts. We are all relatives.

"Brethren, pray for us." (1 Thessalonians 5:25) This is a prayer request. Praying for someone who asks for prayer is being an intercessor. Sometimes the requests are as simple as that, without any specifics. Pray as the Spirit leads you.

Our call greatly involves praying for one another in Christ. Those who follow Yeshua have an enemy. This is an area of prayer and intercession that is powerful and empowers the receiver to overcome.

"Simon, Simon, behold, Satan demanded to have you all sifted like wheat, but I have prayed for you, Simon, that your faith may not fail. And when you have turned back you would strengthen your brothers. 33. But he said, "Lord, I am ready to go with you to prison and to death." 34 Yeshua said, "I tell you, Peter, the rooster will not crow this day, until you deny three times that you know me." 35 And he said to them, "When I sent you out with no moneybag or knapsack or sandals, did you lack anything?" They said, "Nothing." 36 He said to them, "But now let the one who has a moneybag take it, and likewise a knapsack. And let the one who has no sword sell his cloak and buy one. 37 For I tell you that this Scripture must be fulfilled in me: 'And he was numbered with the transgressors.' For what is written about me has its fulfillment." 38 And they said, "Look, Lord, here are two swords." And he said to them, "It is enough." (Luke 22:31-38)

Notice that Satan demanded to sift them like wheat, but permission was in the hands of Yahweh. We need to keep this in mind. Satan needed *permission*.

It was allowed, that sifting, but Yeshua prayed that Peter's faith would not fail even after he transgressed. In other words, he prayed that Peter would not give up and would continue to believe he was loved and forgiven and still belonged to Yeshua.

Yeshua did an obedience check. He reminded Peter of how He provided a way for him when he obeyed. He then asked Peter to do the opposite of what He first told him, and again, Peter obeyed without question and all the more powerfully.

He had not only done the one thing Yeshua said by having one sword, but he also said, "I have two swords."

Yeshua told him that was enough. Peter displayed faith and fortitude and an assurance to Yahweh that though he would soon fail

Yeshua by denying Him, Peter would resoundingly hold to his faith despite his time of weakness.

By Yeshua allowing Satan this sifting, it brought out greater victory in the example of Peter's faith. He accepted redemption, forgiveness, was not hindered by his mistake, and continued to boldly preach the gospel. He knew he was still worthy through Christ.

On the other hand, Judas was paid money when he led the soldiers to Jesus. Later he was so remorseful that he tried to give the money back. The Pharisees would not take it. Judas believed what he did was unforgivable, and he hung himself.

Shame is a silencer and a paralyzer and at times... a killer. But there is nothing too unforgivable or hopeless to be redeemed from by the love of Yahweh and the blood of Yeshua. It has already been shed for us.

Let's not let our own mistakes keep us from being powerful prayer warriors.

What was wrong is forgiven. Repent, hold to your faith, and continue to rest in Yeshua. These are the types of prayers our brothers and sisters in Christ need. Satan likes nothing more than for us to be silenced.

We are told that we can bind Satan. Let's not fear the Enemy and be intimidated, but know the power in Christ and His victory to defeat the Devil's schemes. Don't be running in fear, but be Christ conscious in the shoes of peace, the "Sword of the Spirit which is the Word," and the authority in the Word.

You can bind any evils and ask Yeshua to cast them out to be dealt with to the foot of the Cross where His blood covers. Yeshua has the victory.

He is risen. Praise Him!

Let's consider some of the prayer requests of the disciples. We can look at these and think of one another and pray similar things or ask for prayer like this.

> Finally, brothers, pray for us, that the word of the Lord may speed ahead and be honored, as happened among you, 2 and that we may be delivered from wicked and evil men. For not all have faith. 3 But the Lord is faithful. He will establish you and guard you against the evil one. 4 And we have confidence in the Lord about you, that you are doing and will do the things that we command. 5 May the Lord direct your hearts to the love of Yahweh and to the steadfastness of Christ. (2 Thessalonians 3:1-5)

They recognize the trouble Satan tries to befall on God's people, but they know active prayer for protection and strength is powerful armor to guard against it and proceed in the power of Christ, our victor and Savior.

Yeshua prayed in John 17:15: "I do not ask that you take them out of the world, but that you keep them from the evil one."

> "So Peter was kept in prison, but earnest prayer for him was made to God by the church." (Acts 12:5)

Peter was sustained by prayers from the church of believers.

Ephesians 6:10-20 contains a strong checklist of how to be armed while serving, praying, and proclaiming a life in relationship with Yahweh/YHVH:

> 10 Finally, be strong in the Lord and in the strength of his might. 11 Put on the whole armor of God, that you may be able to stand against the schemes of the devil. 12 For we do not wrestle against flesh and blood, but against the rulers, against

the authorities, against the cosmic powers over this present darkness, against the spiritual forces of evil in the heavenly places.

13 Therefore take up the whole armor of God, that you may be able to withstand in the evil day, and having done all, to stand firm. 14 Stand therefore, having fastened on the belt of truth, and having put on the breastplate of righteousness, 15 and, as shoes for your feet, having put on the readiness given by the gospel of peace. 16 In all circumstances take up the shield of faith, with which you can extinguish all the flaming darts of the evil one; 17 and take the helmet of salvation, and the sword of the Spirit, which is the word of God, 18 praying at all times in the Spirit, with all prayer and supplication.

To that end, keep alert with all perseverance, making supplication for all the saints, 19 and also for me, that words may be given to me in opening my mouth boldly to proclaim the mystery of the gospel, 20 for which I am an ambassador in chains, that I may declare it boldly, as I ought to speak. (Ephesisans 6:10-20)

Note the multiple mentions regarding the Word, our word, our speaking, and our prayers, and the perseverance while being alert. It is all the power of Yahweh given to us in ways of His Spirit and breath upon our own spirit and breath.

This is the power of His Spirit working with ours and the purpose in our lives that goes beyond the Earth and into what is eternal. Life stretches far beyond what we see. We are remarkably made to be able to take part in this kind of eternal life with Yahweh starting here.

These are examples of prayer for divine protection, spiritual strength, and victory over the Enemy. All is achieved through prayer as He answers. There is no reason to doubt it but every reason to speak Yahweh's power and purpose into lives.

Who might you know who isn't comfortable enough or certain

enough or strong enough in faith to put it all before Yahweh and walk into His presence? Deuteronomy 5:4-5 speaks of Moses acknowledging this type of thing with the Israelites as he stood in that place for them:

"4 Yahweh spoke with you face to face at the mountain, out of the midst of the fire, 5 while I stood between Yahweh and you at that time, to declare to you the word of Yahweh. For you were afraid because of the fire, and you did not go up into the mountain."

Some people are afraid or uncomfortable of the fullness of His Holy Spirit and the close connection Yahweh makes in the filling of His Spirit in ways of gifts of tongues, or prophecy or visions. Thus, they don't open themselves up fully to it but rely on others who step into that place.

The fullness of relationship with Yahweh on Earth takes part in many of His gifts. We must be willing to receive it, and in receiving something, we have to take it in.

Just like receiving a present, I have to open up my arms and hands. I have found that open arms and hands in a posture of prayer also opens me up to receive from His Spirit. Receiving those gifts is part of knowing Him more. The more you know Him, the more wonderful life becomes.

My mom had a friend named Betty who prayed for others, and you always knew she was doing it. Betty sent me a Christmas card every year and told me she was praying for me.

She involved herself in many ways in a variety of people's lives: athletes, politicians, top educators, and her friends' children. She was bold and didn't shy away from telling people she was in prayer. She sent Bible verses with every card.

Time moved on, and she developed cancer. She was in a hospice facility, and I went with my mom and my young son to see her. She was aware we were there but didn't have much ability to talk. As my son, then a toddler and getting antsy, seemed ready for me to leave, I asked her if I could pray for her before I left. She nodded.

I held her hand and prayed out loud. My little boy put his hand on her, too. It was a sweet moment.

During that prayer, I had a strange sensation. When I finished, I said to her, "You were praying for me just then, weren't you?"

She nodded again. Even though she no longer had much ability to talk, she could still pray. Selflessly, she didn't just receive my prayer, but she prayed for me in that time of holding hands.

A couple of years later, another man who used to pray for me passed away. He was my Sunday school teacher when I was ten years old. He had remained a part of my life and continued to pray for me into my upper 40's.

After attending his funeral, I decided to visit to his gravesite after all the commotion settled down. To my astonishment, his gravestone was right next to Betty's. They did not know one another, but I stood in that space between them and thanked Yahweh for these people who had prayed for me in my childhood and adulthood.

In that same row, a few grave stones away is my godmother. None of this was planned, none of these people knew one another, but their relationship in my life was all shared in love.

The way that Yahweh brought these people together in that one area of the cemetery is an outstanding message of the power of love, prayer, and God's purposes in relationship and the importance of a life well-lived in Him.

The eternal impact of prayer in all of its forms and purposes is without limit. Sometimes we get to see a glimpse of His plan. Other times, we have to trust His plan. Your purpose is in His plan. Free yourself to be more open in areas of faith-filled prayer for others. Your invitation to "come" is always open.

There are lists of Bible verses of Yahweh answering, responding, receiving, and accepting prayers that you can search for online. Prayer is conversation. Answering is part of His relationship-building. It is also a place to see unanswered prayers and know that His will and thoughts are Holy and that we can trust Him in that part, too.

Knowing Jesus, "27 Bible Verses about God Answers Prayer"

OpenBibleInfo.com, "God Answering Prayers"

CHAPTER THIRTEEN
REVEALING THE POWER OF BLESSING!

BLESSED TO BE A BLESSING

This wonderful path that Yahweh has led us on leads to greater freedom of who we are in Him and the power He produces in partnering with us and through us. The fullness and purpose of you in Him and Him in you really is a new life and an abundant life. Let's continue learning as He reveals more of Himself.

The area of blessing has been a life-changer for me. I was recently made aware of it in a book written by Rolf Garborg called *The Family Blessing*. It opened me up to an awareness I hadn't known before. I began studying blessing further and putting it into practice in a variety of ways with the understanding of breath behind it.

Let's start with the definition of blessing.

From The American Heritage Dictionary of the English Language Fifth Edition

---

"1. The act of one that blesses. 2. A short prayer said before or after a meal; grace. 3. Something promoting or contributing to happiness, well-being, or prosperity..."

From the Free Merriam-Webster Dictionary:

"1. to hallow or consecrate by religious rite or word. 2. : to hallow with the sign of the cross. 3. : to invoke divine care for <bless your heart>"

"the act or words of a person who blesses. 2. a special favor, mercy, or benefit: the blessings of liberty."

Notice that a blessing over a meal is called "grace." Grace is a blessing.

The Hebrew word for "bless" is *berekh* which literally means "to kneel." A *berakah* is a "blessing" but more literally the bringing of a gift to another on a bended knee. Below are the Hebrew words and their letters.

This is for bless, which also means knee: ברך

This is for blessing: ברכה

We see in bless to blessing, reading from right to left, that the blessing comes with the Hebrew letter *hey* or *hei*: ה

Definitions state that *HEY* represents the number five. It appears twice in the sacred Name of YHVH. It is therefore a symbol of Divinity and divine breath YHVH.

Did you catch that?

Divine *breath* appears two times in His Name.

YHVH/Yahweh in Hebrew letters is: יהוה

We know He breathed life into man at Creation, and we have learned that He breathed His Holy Spirit into us for the eternal when Yeshua breathed on them and said, "Receive my Spirit." Divine breath occurred two times for new life.

The Lord had said to Abram, "Go from your country, your people and your father's household to the land I will show you. 2 "I will make you into a great nation, and I will bless you; I will make your name great, and you will be a blessing. 3 I will bless those who bless you, and whoever curses you I will curse; and all peoples on earth will be blessed through you. (Genesis 12:1-3)

This is a prophetic message of what will come when Abram believes and obeys. It is filled with blessings, and here you see the importance and tie of blessings from YHVH. What God pours out in blessing, Abram will pour out in blessing.

A little later, Melchizedek blesses Abram. His origin and departure is unknown and speculated upon, but it confirms the blessing on Abram: "and he blessed Abram, saying, "Blessed be Abram by God Most High, Creator of heaven and earth. 20 And blessed be God Most High, who delivered your enemies into your hand." (Genesis 14:19-20)

Abram obeyed YHVH in leaving his father's tent to places unknown. YHVH saw his faithfulness, and this is what followed:

When Abram was ninety-nine years old, Yahweh/YHVH appeared to him and said, "I am God Almighty; walk before me faithfully and be blameless. 2 Then I will make my covenant between me and you and will greatly increase your numbers."

3 Abram fell facedown, and God said to him, 4 "As for me,

this is my covenant with you: You will be the father of many nations. 5 No longer will you be called Abram; your name will be Abraham, for I have made you a father of many nations. 6 I will make you very fruitful; I will make nations of you, and kings will come from you.

7 I will establish my covenant as an everlasting covenant between me and you and your descendants after you for the generations to come, to be your God and the God of your descendants after you. 8 The whole land of Canaan, where you now reside as a foreigner, I will give as an everlasting possession to you and your descendants after you; and I will be their God." (Genesis 17:1-8)

Upon God's blessing:

אברם - Abram
אַבְרָהָם - Abraham
שרי - Sarai
שרה - Sarah

God added the ה (*hey*) to their names, as evidence of His breath of blessing and abundant life. Sarai's name had ended with a *yud*, which is representative of a strong hand/arm of power. Yahweh removed that from her name and gave His breath in its place.

Breath is life, and soon she and Abraham would bear a son in their old age. He would be the first of their descendants as numerous as the grains of sand.

Yahweh's use of blessing is His love upon us, His favor upon us, and His grace upon us.

Blessings are spoken over us. Yahweh spoke to Moses and conveyed what He wanted spoken over His people. The love in these words shows the fullness of His love. Church leaders often say this blessing, but I have to confess, I didn't fully appreciate that these were YHVH's own words upon me. This may sound familiar to you, too:

---

22 Yahweh spoke to Moses, saying, 23 "Speak to Aaron and his sons, saying, Thus you shall bless the people of Israel: you shall say to them,

24 YHVH/Yahweh bless you and keep you;

25 YHVH/Yahweh make his face to shine upon you and be gracious to you;

26 YHVH/Yahweh lift up his countenance upon you and give you peace.

27 So shall they put My name upon the people of Israel, and I will bless them." (Numbers 6:22)

His name written in Hebrew is YHVH and is translated to "Lord." What we are really saying is, "YHVH bless you and keep you."

His name is upon His people, and by this we are blessed. Placing His name upon us makes us children.

Yahweh gave us His name. He asked us to speak it. Man decided it was too sacred to say or even write out.

Because of that, the Enemy interfered in our relationship with Him and also removed the power of His name on us and over situations. It is time to know and speak His name. "Lord" is not His name. It is more of a title, and worse, the same word is given to Baal, an idol that was worshiped.

In today's society, most children take their father's name and sometimes a combination of their mother and father's name. This brings in inheritance. Now that we have a fuller understanding of the power of words and the importance of names, to have these spoken over us in His name humbles us and covers us with love at the same time.

Hear the words of being kept in blessing. Think of His face looking upon you as it shines with light and smiling, radiant, grace.

As He lifts His countenance upon us, we can understand that better. Countenance also means his face includes a facial expression. Verb definitions of countenance have included favor, support, approval, uphold and tolerate.

This would have to be a smile. This is His favor over you and for you as His.

It wasn't our idea to speak out and hope He would do this for us. These are His words to be spoken over us even before Christ came to Earth for His followers. He has always looked upon us with grace, favor, approval, support, and with that love, He tolerates our errors. He is gracious to us in His blessing.

It is the love of a Father with His name on you. This kind of blessing of love, favor, and grace gives you peace. Only He gives a peace that can't be explained, but in our understanding of the fullness of His love for us, there is an added peace. We don't have to strive for it.

Our actions matter to Him in way of blessing others as He blesses us to be a blessing. When we realize His love, it helps to turn us away from a life of searching in unhealthy ways because we have found the source of what we have long searched for. Then we want to share it with others.

Now, when I hear this blessing spoken over us from a spiritual leader, I close my eyes and hold out my hands to receive it. I want the fullness of it.

Let's look at the Name of YHVH/Yahweh again:

יהוה

Reading from right to left, the small symbol on the right is called *yud*. This is an English phonetic spelling of it.

It represents the number ten and also includes power, hand and creation; which is the power of God's own hand.

Next is the *hey*, then *vav,* and another *hey*.

The *hey* meaning includes "divine breath" and also the number five. Five is a number associated with grace.

The *vav* has a couple of meanings.

It is a symbol for man as it represents the number six. On the sixth day, God created man. It is also symbolic as a tent peg. The tent peg is part of a temporary dwelling. (*Hebrew for Christians*, John J Parsons, Chabad.org)

This is what we see when YHVH/Yahweh answers when asked who He is. His response: "I Am."

Hebrew linguists say that YHVH comes from the verb *havah*, meaning "to be."

I see some things in this. I see His powerful hand forming Creation and us from dust in the *yud*.

His breath breathed as life in the first *hey* as He breathed into man.

I see man or the Son of Man in the *vav* and then... the breath of Life in the Spirit that was the Holy Spirit of Yeshua in the second *hey*.

- The man in the center, or *vav* is Christ, as also the Son of Man. The *vav* also represents a tent peg or stake as symbolic of going into each hand of Christ as He hung on the cross, and that the peg was like the tent peg for the temporary dwelling place or home.
- Christ dwelled with us and is spoken in the name *Immanuel* which means "God with us." Christ in a human body was His physical, temporary dwelling place here amongst us.
- Following the *vav* is a second *hey*. It is the breath that Yeshua breathed as dwelling with us and in us through His Spirit. He said to the disciples, "'Receive my Spirit,' and with that, He breathed on them."

Every time you see LORD in uppercase letters, it is translating

YHVH. In Scripture, His name is presented around 6,800 times this way. I have begun to pray to Him as YHVH more often, especially in my understanding of His power in it.

This one name represents the full Trinity.

- Isaiah 9:6 prophesies of Christ, but it is also telling in the fullness of His name as YHVH: "For to us a child is born, to us a son is given, and the government will be on his shoulders. And he will be called Wonderful Counselor, Mighty God, Everlasting Father, Prince of Peace..."
- Mighty God can be seen in the **Y**ud.
- Everlasting Father as the first breath into Adam in the **H**ey
- Prince of Peace in the body of Christ as Son of man and God in the **V**av
- Wonderful Counselor in the Spirit that Jesus breathed in the second **H**ey

Or, YHVH.

As we speak the blessing of the LORD/YHVH, it is in the abundance, power, and fullness of His Trinity.

These symbols captivate me. If the *hey* is equal to the number five, we see our five fingers with each breath, too. "You go before me and follow me. You place your hand of blessing on my head." (Psalm 139:5 NLT)

Blessing often comes with the placement of hands on the one being blessed or raised hands over the ones being blessed. The power of the blessing is extended. We see Yeshua do this in Mark 10:13-16:

> People were bringing little children to Yeshua to have him touch them, but the disciples rebuked them. When Yeshua saw this, he was indignant. He said to them, "Let the little children come to me, and do not hinder them, for the kingdom of God belongs to such as these. 15 I tell you the truth, anyone who will not

receive the kingdom of God like a little child will never enter it." 16 And he took the children in his arms, put his hands on them and blessed them.

∼

A friend sent me a message one morning. She told me to read Luke 24:45. This is what it says: "then he opened their minds to understand the Scriptures."

She wrote on, "May He do this to you as well." She blessed me with this.

> "But you are a chosen people, a royal priesthood, a holy nation, God's special possession, that you may declare the praises of him who called you out of darkness into his wonderful light." (1 Peter 2:9)

We are given the ability to speak blessings over others. It does not have to come from an ordained leader from higher theological learning. YHVH has ordained you!

As God spoke to Moses and told of the nation of Israel, the Hebrew people, He gave them a priesthood and with it the ability to bless:

I am aware of people who were called priests and they committed horrible sins against others. That was not the will of YHVH. Don't let the sins of others destroy the true intention and definition YHVH gave to being part of a royal priesthood. Satan will do many things to try and destroy our relationship with YHVH.

Let's look at God's Word again.

> "Now if you obey me fully and keep my covenant, then out of

all nations you will be my treasured possession. Although the whole earth is mine, you will be for me a kingdom of priests and a holy nation.' These are the words you are to speak to the Israelites." (Exodus 19:5-6)

God has given both Jew and Gentile the priesthood, and in the priesthood is the ability of blessing.

What has blessed me further this morning from the message I received from my friend is that she told me to read all of Chapter 24. I got to verses 50 and 51 and found a beautiful example of Yeshua blessing as He raised His hands. This was the last thing that He did for us while being here in physical form, even as He ascended to Heaven. Blessing is *huge*.

Here are the verses:

When he had led them out to the vicinity of Bethany, he lifted up his hands and blessed them. While he was blessing them, he left them and was taken up into heaven. (Luke 24:5-51)

This is a remarkably powerful insight to the importance of blessing. Surely His blessing continues upon us from Heaven.

How good is YHVH to make this abundantly clear right as I am writing this? We praise you, YHVH, for desiring your message to be known to us and making it clear!.

Blessing and grace share the same synonym. A synonym is another word that essentially means the same thing. The synonym for both blessing and grace is favor.

Blessing is speaking favor into someone's life. Grace from Yahweh is mercy and love, and it is given to us not because of anything that we have done. This is favor. Favor is defined as kindness and liking. It is good to know that YHVH likes us.

Yeshua blessed. He reached out His hand, touching the children and blessing them. It is an extension of Himself upon them.

Touching is connecting. Reaching toward someone is an attempt at connecting. Yeshua extended His hands, reaching out more of Himself in blessing during His ascension to Heaven. This is a gesture of connection.

When one waves to another, it is a communication of connection. When our children spot us in an audience during one of their performances, they wave, and we wave back to them. Connecting.

How many times have you seen concerts where front-row fans are reaching out their arms or hands toward the performer? They reach out, hoping to connect.

A blessing given by extended hands is connecting. If you receive the touch of that performer or that professional player, you feel favor. You reached out to that player or performer because you felt favor for them, too.

The Hebrew people understood the importance of blessing. The history of their blessings is extensive and continues today.

A strong example of the importance of receiving a blessing and giving a blessing is found in the example of Isaac, the father, and Jacob and Esau, his two sons. In Genesis 27:1-40, Isaac is nearing death. He is old and blind and knows it is time to pass on the family blessing to his oldest son.

Before the big event, Isaac asked Esau to go and hunt and prepare his favorite food. He favored Esau's abilities and strengths as a skilled and knowledgeable hunter. Esau's mother also knew what Isaac's favorite food was, and she knew how to prepare the food exactly the way he liked it.

Esau's mother had favor for Jacob over Esau. She wanted Jacob to receive the blessing. She planned to use Isaac's blindness/weakness and put Jacob there to receive the blessing instead. She told Jacob that she would make the food the way Isaac liked it and that she wanted Jacob to pretend he was Esau and act like he had prepared it.

Jacob knew it was not his birthright to receive the blessing. He feared that when his father found out that he had lied, his father would curse him, but his mother insisted and said if there is any curse for misleading the blessing, she said to let it come upon her. This relieved some of Jacob's guilt and fear, and it also emphasized the favor his mother felt for him.

Isaac would place his hands upon him in the blessing, and Jacob knew that he would not feel like his brother who was much more hairy. His mother wrapped Jacob's arms and the back of his neck with the hair from goatskin. She also had him wear Esau's clothes.

As Jacob served his dad and claimed to be Esau, Isaac wasn't certain. It wasn't until Jacob kissed him and Isaac smelled the familiar scent of Esau's clothing on him that he was convinced.

In that nearness and deeper identification did Isaac decide to go ahead and bless him, believing it really was Esau as he said, "Ah! The smell of my son is like the smell of the outdoors, which YHVH has blessed!"

He repeated the same portion of blessing that God gave to his father, Abraham: "All who curse you will be cursed, and all who bless you will be blessed."

I noticed the betrayal of a kiss, which was the same way that Judas betrayed Yeshua. Again, the connection of all Christ did for us for the sake of forgiveness reaches me deeply.

When Esau returned and came to his father for his blessing, it says that upon recognizing Esau, Isaac trembled uncontrollably. He told Esau he had given his blessing to Jacob and that the blessing must stand.

His words were out. One did not go back on their word. The word carried life, favor, blessing, and it mattered. Once it was spoken, it was.

His upset for the misplaced blessing made him tremble uncontrollably. It goes on to say that when Isaac told him what had happened, Esau lets out a loud and bitter cry. He begged, "Bless me, too!"

The blessing was real. The words had tangible power. He replied to Esau, "He has taken away your blessing."

Isaac shared what the consequences of life would be for Esau because of the blessing given to Jacob. In verse 38, Esau pleaded, "But do you have only one blessing? Oh my father, bless me, too!" Then Esau broke down and wept.

A blessing meant everything. Words were sacred. A father's blessing is of high value, as is a blessing in the name of Yahweh, Father of all. As Satan attempts to curse with insecurity and inferiority, the blessing of Yahweh counteracts the curse.

Opposite of insecurity; it gives Security in a blessing, "The Lord bless you and keep you."

Opposite of inferiority; it gives Favor in a blessing, "The Lord make His face shine upon you and be gracious to you."

In the Jewish culture, there are blessings of many kinds. They are often noticed at a pivotal place: at the end of one thing and the beginning of another.

Baptism is also a place like this. It marks the end of one life and a birth into a new life. When Yahweh's *Ruah*/Holy Spirit descended and landed on Yeshua, Yahweh said, "This is My Son, in whom I am well pleased."

The Father/Creator/Yahweh also did this to Yeshua when He was transfigured. It was another pivotal place revealing the everlasting and eternal life of Yeshua in His transfigured body.

In that newness of life revealed, God as Father spoke again from a bright cloud in Matthew 17:5: "While he was still speaking, a bright cloud covered them, and a voice from the cloud said, 'This is my Son, whom I love; with him I am well pleased. Listen to him!'"

Here are a few of the pivotal places of common Jewish blessing:

- There is a blessing for a woman who has just given birth, whether the child lives or not. She is blessed for having carried life, and as that time has ended for her, her life is different no matter what for the life she had carried. Women never forget the ones they delivered or miscarried.
- There are blessings for seasons and feasts that mark the calendars moving from one time to another.

- There is the Sabbath blessing that is done at the end of each week and the beginning of the next. It is a blessing over the household and family. My favorite example of it is in *Fiddler on the Roof*. The women of the family light the two candles that represent to keep and to remember the Sabbath as in the Torah and Ten Commandments.

Women light these because they are thought of as the connection of keeping the spirit of the home. Men may light them if a woman isn't present, but either way, the candles must be lit within eighteen minutes of sunset. Again, in Hebrew, eighteen is a very important number and represents *Chai,* which means "life."

The time of rest in the Sabbath is a gift, and it is a time meant to be well in the peace, grace, favor, and goodness of the presence of Yahweh without doing any work. Through Him the body finds restoration and refreshing, as well as the mind and spirit. The old week is shed and the new week begins in Him.

So was the work of Creation. So is blessing. The Sabbath is the blessing of the seventh day, and it is in reverence of Yahweh's first blessing in the Scriptures: "So God blessed the seventh day and made it holy, because on it God rested from all his work that he had done in creation." (Genesis 2:3)

When Yeshua came, He became our Sabbath rest. He fulfilled all law, and now we receive a continual refreshing and restoration of body, mind, soul, and spirit while shedding the old because He makes all things new.

The Jewish people have blessings for every feast and holiday, for meals, for trips, for weddings, and for age passages as in *Bar Mitzvahs, Bat Mitzvahs,* and *Brit Milah,* the circumcision of an eight-day old male. The number eight in Hebrew represents a new beginning, and the *Brit Milah* signifies the covenant of removal of flesh between their infant child and God, as they bless the life of this child.

They say blessings when they see a rainbow, when they hear thunder, when they are recovering from illness, when beholding something beautiful in nature, when seeing a Torah sage, when the reading of the Torah, when entering a synagogue, when leaving a synagogue, when dedicating a home.

There are blessings for healing, strength, wisdom, experiencing a miracle or deliverance, seeing the ocean, self-acceptance, anointing with oil, their country, freedom, and the Earth. It is endless. There are wonderful blessings in the Word of Yahweh from Genesis to Revelation.

Another friend of mine recently sent me a lovely blessing that she had been looking for. It was one that a wife could say over her husband. John Ferret, with *Light of Menorah Ministries*, sent her this:

> "Bless my husband who does not walk in the counsel of the wicked, nor stand in the path of sinners, nor sit in the seat of scoffers! But his delight is in the Torah of the LORD/ *Yahweh*. May he be like a tree firmly planted by streams of water, which yields its fruit in its season and its leaf does not wither; and in whatever he does, he prospers.
>
> Bless my husband who fears YOU, *Avaynoonu*, our Father who walks in the ways of Rabbi Yeshua as a *talmid*, a disciple. May it be, my husband, that when you shall eat of the fruit of your hands, you will be happy and it will be well with you. May I, your wife be like a fruitful vine within our house, your children like olive plants around our table. Behold, for thus shall the man be blessed, who fears the LORD/*Yahweh*.
>
> The LORD/*Yahweh* bless you from Zion, and may you see the prosperity of Jerusalem all the days of your life. Indeed, may you see your children's children. Peace be upon Israel, upon His people, and all of us of the nations grafted in to the Olive Tree by the blood of Messiah!

Lord/Yahweh, I thank You for Your blessing of this man to me. I ask that You bless him and remove all fear and doubt from his heart and mind. Grant him Your shalom, Your peace that surpasses all understanding. I ask that You guide his steps and guard his path from Satan. Let him know that I am committed to You, and I am committed to him. In the name of Yeshua Ha Mashiach, Jesus the Messiah, I pray. Amen."

My friend also shared that this man blesses his wife with the words from Proverbs 31:10-31.

In Rolf Garborg's book, *The Family Blessing*, Rolf describes how he chose to bless his children at night before they went to sleep.

He said that it was a quiet time at the end of the day, and if there were troubles in that day, he had to let them go because blessing is difficult if you are holding a grudge or are upset with the person you are intending to bless. Removing any and all barriers, he blessed his children.

I bless my son in the morning before he leaves for school. I say a prayer for him, and then as he gets his backpack on, I place my hands on his head and say the blessing from Numbers: "Yahweh bless you and keep you, Samuel. Yahweh make His face shine on you and be gracious to you, may He lift up His countenance upon you and give you His peace, in the Name of the Father, Son and Holy Spirit."

Then I kiss him on his head and tell him I love him, and he runs out the door. I often stand in the window and lift my hand in blessing toward his bus as it pulls away.

When he has been running late and we are scurrying to get his things ready and I haven't given him his blessing yet, he will tip his head toward me and chase me around with his head down yelling, "Mom, my blessing, my blessing!"

He doesn't want to leave without it. To him, it is as urgent as getting his backpack on. I say it as fast as I can, and he runs out the door.

On days when I don't have him with me, I call him on the phone and say his blessing. Sometimes if I haven't called him yet, he will call me. He wants his prayers and blessing.

Rolf also wrote about the impact of speaking well into his children's lives as he shares great personal stories. I began to call my son "Super Sam." He loves it. He often smiles when I call him that, and he behaves more confidently when I do.

I had called him that from time to time, but I really stepped it up when I read how Rolf began calling his daughter a sweet nickname that impacts her positively still today as well as her children. It was contagious in a good way.

Negative nicknames leave a mark. Most all of us can recall one from our childhood. It could have been a sibling, another child, or a parent or adult. Those negative words linger.

As you think of them, think of the person that said them, forgive them in your heart, and pray a blessing for that person. It is healing and freeing for you. I know it can be hard, but it is worth the effort. It is another place to be healed and a place for truth for who Yahweh says you are in Him. He calls you Beloved.

In knowledge of these things, begin to think of positive names for the people you love. Speak well into their lives. Good words are a blessing. We don't always see an instant result, but eventually it will come.

In *The Family Blessing*, Rolf tells a Zig Ziglar story about bamboo.

A bamboo sprout takes a few years before it begins to gain any real height, and one can cultivate around it before you see much growth. Then suddenly, in some cases, it can grow thirty inches in less than twenty-four hours.

Blessing and prayers for our children can be like that. You can spend a lot of time in these areas before you see growth.

Don't give up. There is never any regret for having remained committed and devoted to speaking well into someone's life.

CHAPTER FOURTEEN
WHEN IT'S UP TO US

THE CHOICE

> "Today I have given you the choice between life and death, between blessings and curses. Now I call on heaven and earth to witness the choice you make. Oh, that you would choose life, so that you and your descendants might live!" (Deuteronomy 30:19)

To me, it doesn't get any clearer than that: a choice between life and death. The blessing of following His commands. Our words can kill, or our words can make one thrive and live. Blessing and cursing.

How often do we curse ourselves by saying we are bound to make a mistake or that we can't do something? Or worse yet, we will never change? What we can say is that Yeshua will keep us from falling, and He will change us. By His strength, we can do what He set us out to do.

He set us out to love, to bless, and to be blessed so our descendants might live. It is a path of life for our children, our family, and others so that those following us walk into blessing. It means proclaiming Yeshua's life into their lives.

Yeshua took our sin, our shame, and our curses. "Christ hath redeemed us from the curse of the law, being made a curse for us: for it is written, cursed is every one that hangeth on a tree." (Galatians 3:13)

Think about that. Are we cursing ourselves?

The words of the Law or commandments allowed us to see our imperfections and our sin. The Law revealed sin. None of us have been able to keep all the commandments. Only Yeshua remained sinless in all of the commandments. This was why He was the only perfect sacrifice to pay for our sins.

The first curse comes from Yahweh upon the land for our sake. I see mercy even in this time. Hardship has come, but ultimately the curse was put on the land for our benefit.

Genesis 3:17-18 NKJV reads:

Then to Adam He said, "Because you have heeded the voice of your wife, and have eaten from the tree of which I commanded you, saying, 'You shall not eat of it': "Cursed is the ground for your sake; In toil you shall eat of it all the days of your life. 18 Both thorns and thistles it shall bring forth for you, and you shall eat the herb of the field.

But Yeshua absorbed this curse, too: "And the soldiers twisted together a crown of thorns and put it on his head and arrayed him in a purple robe." (John 19:2)

The crown placed on His head in mockery was a crown of thorns—the curse upon His head.

The power of this kind of love from our Father can drop us to our knees. And there, we receive His blessing of grace, love, mercy, favor, keeping, and life. "For God so loved the world that He gave His one and only Son, so that whoever believes in Him will not perish but have everlasting life." (John 3:16)

As He has shared the greatest example of love and kindness, He asks us to do the same. As He does, we are to do.

> "Make allowance for each other's faults, and forgive anyone who offends you. Remember, Yahweh forgave you, so you must forgive others." (Colossians 3:13 NLT)
>
> "Bless those who persecute you; bless and do not curse." (Romans 12:14)

I want to reemphasize that: "Bless and do not curse."

The first place to start is to forgive yourself. This will free you to receive fully and walk in Yahweh's blessing/life for you. If you are walking with your own self-cursing/death, you are missing out on the fullness of life of Yahweh's blessings.

If it is hard for you, then ask Yeshua to help you see that He took everything on the cross for you. Now when He looks at you, He sees you without condemnation. He took it all, and it is buried with His death for you.

As Graham Cooke said at an Arise conference in Minnesota, "Stop being a grave robber!"

We don't need to dig up the negative past things we've done. Yeshua took it all to the grave in your place. Live in freedom. He died so you may live. He came back to life to show you His glory, power, and the defeat of sin and death and that He is giving you a new life, too.

The Creator/Yahweh has given us simple instructions in His Word and hasn't left us fending for ourselves on how to live. His desire is for us to live in His same nature, which is blessing.

> "Finally, all of you, live in harmony with one another; be sympathetic, love as brothers, be compassionate and humble. 9 Do not repay evil with evil or insult with insult, but with blessing, because to this you were called so that you may inherit a blessing." (1 Peter 3:8-9)

As Rolf wrote, "Forgiveness and Blessing go hand in hand."

∼

As I was on my blessing spree, I shared it with my daughter. We were driving by an area of town that had become old and empty. Things had come and gone, and one location kept having failed business after failed business.

I told her I was praying blessings over those places and that God's favor would come and the businesses would thrive. She looked at me skeptically and said, "I think you are taking this blessing thing a little too far."

In her defense, she has had two years of Bible school and has a strong faith, but so few of us have been taught the fullness of blessing.

A little over a year later, I remembered our conversation as we were driving by the same area. She was in the car with me. Gone were the broken-down buildings, and in their place stood a new restaurant. There is a new road waiting for more businesses, and in the building that kept having failed businesses was a new store called Droolin' Moose.

You can tell we live in Minnesota.

It is a chocolate shop with another part of their store used for screen-printing parties. I reminded her of how I had been speaking blessing over those places as she looked at the new businesses. She said she had never been in the chocolate shop yet, and I told her that neither had I. With a sharp turn, we pulled into the parking lot.

Inside, we sampled all of their delicious chocolates. I couldn't help but tell the woman working there how I had prayed blessings for them ever since they opened. She responded back just as happily and said, "We are doing so well that we are opening a second store!"

I was thrilled to learn about Yahweh's goodness and blessing for them.

A few months later my mom called me and said she saw a Droolin' Moose store opening up right by where she lived. She had known this story and was thrilled that their next store was right in her neighborhood. Now they have a third store and are still growing.

This isn't any power that I had, but it is the power of our God-given gift of words and the power in His blessing. He has given us a life to do as He does.

One of the most life-changing times of blessing for me was in 2012 when I was driving my car down a suburban road. Coming up the other side on horseback were about thirty people dressed in regalia and the Chief in his headdress.

I pulled over, stopped my car, rolled down my window, and extended my hand in blessing over those riding. The rider in front noticed and nodded at me. I felt his blessing.

Later on the news, I learned they were riders going along the old Dakota trail that led to a mission site and Fort Snelling. It was in honor and preparation for the 150th anniversary of the mass hanging in Mankato of the Dakota thirty-eight and two at Fort Snelling.

When I learned they were riding under the mantra of "Forgive Everyone Everything," I was stunned. I knew new life was coming. With forgiveness comes new life. I have watched it unfold.

Five years later, in 2017, Mankato held a Dakota honor event, and the Mayor of the City and Governor officially welcomed the Dakota back. The Dakota began the change by forgiving before anyone had asked to be forgiven. Just like Yeshua. Blessing has begun.

Not all blessings start out feeling good. Sometimes they come with pain first, but Yahweh promises to use all things for good. We can look at the blessing of favor spoken to Mary and what would come for her.

As so much good was going to come, she would also have to endure watching her son die on a cross. Yet the promise of His Kingdom never ending was part of her blessing.

> But the angel said to her, "Do not be afraid, Mary, you have found favor with God. 31 You will be with child and give birth to a son, and you are to give him the name Yeshua. 32 He will be great and will be called the Son of the Most High. And the LORD God will give him the throne of his father David, 33 and he will reign over the house of Jacob forever; his kingdom will never end." (Luke 1:30-33)

Mary received additional blessing, and so did Yeshua by Elizabeth, who was filled with *Ruah Ha Kodesh*/Holy Spirit when Mary came and greeted her. In that moment, the baby in Elizabeth (John the Baptist) leaped. "In a loud voice she exclaimed: 'Blessed are you among women, and blessed is the child you will bear!'" (Luke 1:42)

Even as curses are spoken, Yahweh turns them into blessing. Multiple times in Scripture we see the example of the curse of Balaam being used as a blessing by Yahweh:

> "However, Yahweh your God would not listen to Balaam but turned the curse into a blessing for you, because Yahweh your God loves you." (Deuteronomy 3:25)
>
> "But I would not listen to Balaam, so he blessed you again and again, and I delivered you out of his hand." (Joshua 24:10)
>
> "For they had not provided the Israelites with food and water in the wilderness. Instead, they hired Balaam to curse them, though our God turned the curse into a blessing." (Nehemiah 13:2)

Graham Cooke gave me permission to share this story of his. Once while traveling on an airplane, the man seated next to him proclaimed that he was a Satanist and that he was there to curse Graham.

Graham, being completely confident in God, decided to get comfortable. He got up and got a beverage from the beverage cart, asked the Satanist if he could get him one and then came back to his seat. Graham got a pen and paper out and told him he was ready to hear and write down the curse.

The Satanist proceeded to curse him, and when he had finished, Graham expressed his disappointment. He told the Satanist that he knows God turns every curse into a blessing and that he was really hoping for more and to try again.

Eventually Graham told the man he was really bad at being a Satanist and that he wasn't on the plane to curse him, but he was on that plane to know God. Graham tells this story so well, and if you ever get a chance to hear him or read any of his books, you will be blessed.

Another area that is commonly referred to as the "beatitudes" is not always defined in plain language. "Beatitudes" means "supreme blessedness." These are blessings spoken by Yeshua. Look at them again. Not all of them start out as good, but all are turned into blessings.

Now when Yeshua saw the crowds, he went up on a mountainside and sat down. His disciples came to him, 2 and he began to teach them. He said:

3 "Blessed are the poor in spirit,

for theirs is the kingdom of heaven.

4 Blessed are those who mourn,

for they will be comforted.

5 Blessed are the meek,

for they will inherit the earth.

6 Blessed are those who hunger and thirst for righteousness,

for they will be filled.

7 Blessed are the merciful,

for they will be shown mercy.

8 Blessed are the pure in heart,
for they will see God.
9 Blessed are the peacemakers,
for they will be called children of God.
10 Blessed are those who are persecuted because of righteousness,
for theirs is the kingdom of heaven.
11 "Blessed are you when people insult you, persecute you and falsely say all kinds of evil against you because of me. 12 Rejoice and be glad, because great is your reward in heaven, for in the same way they persecuted the prophets who were before you." (Matthew 5:1-11)

Blessing is powerful and important. In our worship of YHVH we see numerous times in the Psalms where David understands the greatest thing one can give is blessing, and so he speaks again and again of blessing YHVH in his worship of Him. It is giving his best back to YHVH.

"Bless YHVH, O my soul: and all that is within me, bless his holy name." (Psalm 103:1)

Yeshua did much blessing, but He also uttered curses. He cursed a fig tree for not bearing fruit. This is also a symbolic example. It was not season for the fig to bear fruit, yet Yeshua knew that the importance of fruit when another is hungry in season or not, was vital.

We should always bear fruit. Fruit is the produce that multiplies with seeds for more. If we are fruitful as one of Yahweh's people, we are a blessing.

In earlier parts of this book we have read where words and what we say are the fruit of our lips. It is good to be able to have something good to offer someone else when they need it. Read these passages form Mark 11:

> On the following day, when they came from Bethany, he was hungry. 13 And seeing in the distance a fig tree in leaf, he went to see if he could find anything on it. When he came to it, he found nothing but leaves, for it was not the season for figs. 14 And he said to it, "May no one ever eat fruit from you again." And his disciples heard it. The curse was given merely by His words and they were heard and witnessed. (Mark 11:12-14)
>
> As they passed by in the morning, they saw the fig tree withered away to its roots. 21 And Peter remembered and said to him, "Rabbi, look! The fig tree that you cursed has withered." 22 And Yeshua answered them, "Have faith in God. 23 Truly, I say to you, whoever says to this mountain, 'Be taken up and thrown into the sea,' and does not doubt in his heart, but believes that what he says will come to pass, it will be done for him. 24 Therefore I tell you, whatever you ask in prayer, believe that you have received it, and it will be yours. 25 And whenever you stand praying, forgive, if you have anything against anyone, so that your Father also who is in heaven may forgive you your trespasses." (Mark 11:20-25)

The fig tree was withered at its roots. Remember, that in order to wither at the roots, it must be cut off from water. The supply of its life was cut off. Yeshua showed the power of words and believing as well as the power of words in prayer by faith. He showed that God will do whatever you ask in prayer and that you have received it.

This is a huge teaching of the power of life in words through Yeshua and faith in Him as the Giver.

Equally important, He brings forgiveness into this time of prayer. Forgiveness is the key to the full nearness of the Creator/Yahweh in all parts of your life. Don't let grievances and unforgiveness take up a place that could be filled with a greater fullness of God.

If anyone knows you are holding grudges, bitterness, anger, and resentment, your words will mean nothing as if you were a branch with leaves without fruit.

We sometimes call fruit "produce." Yeshua shows the importance of producing fruit and the value of life in doing so. How can you produce fruit for others by the life of your words? Are there hungry people longing the fruit of your blessings, prayers, loving words, or shared Scripture?

A terrible event happened in Minnesota on Dec. 26th, 1862. It was the largest mass execution performed by the U.S. Government. On that date, like I mentioned earlier, thirty-eight Dakotas were hung in Mankato, Minnesota and plus two more at Fort Snelling following the Dakota War.

While slaves were being freed under the presidency of Abraham Lincoln, battles and wars raged over the state of Minnesota as settlers and pioneers took over the land.

Minnesota is a Dakota word meaning, "Sky-tinted water." The root *mni* (also spelled *mini* or *minne*) means "water." In Hebrew, this would have equated to *shamayim* for "sky/heaven" and *mayim* for "water." The Dakota demonstrated the name to early settlers by dropping milk in water and calling it *mni sota*.

I lived along the trails of the Dakota and up the hill from the Minnesota River. My home backed against a land once lived on by a Dakota named Cloudman with his tribe. A man named Gideon Pond was a missionary to the Dakotas and acted as a go-between for the army at Fort Snelling. Cloudman and the Dakota had a good friendship with Gideon Pond.

During that prayer ride I witnessed, they stopped at the preserved mission site of Gideon Pond and prayed. I was blessed to have been driving my car as they were riding horseback toward me, up the hill of their old trail, now paved in asphalt.

The clapping of horse hooves filled the air. The reverence overwhelmed my spirit. On that cold Dec. 26th at the honoring, their breath and the breath of the horses rose in the air.

They were letting go of any and all bitterness. They rode to the place of the hangings, now a park named "Reconciliation." The beauty of this forgiveness has reached me to a depth like nothing else that I have experienced personally.

In humility, gentility and genuine forgiveness, they rode and upon arriving, read the names of those that were hung.

They were breaking the generations of loss and hurt and bitterness by bringing with them forgiveness for everything and everyone. Young and old, male and female; they rode together.

The United States has twenty-eight states that are Native American names or words. The realization of what was lost is vast. But I do believe with all of my heart that blessing is coming. As we have learned, "Forgiveness and blessing go hand in hand."

"We work hard with our own hands. When we are cursed, we bless; when we are persecuted, we endure it..." (1 Corinthians 4:12)

In Galatians 3:13-14, Paul talks about Yeshua taking the curse: "Christ has redeemed us from the curse of the law, being made a curse for us: for it is written, Cursed is every one that hangs on a tree: 14 That the blessing of Abraham might come on the Gentiles through Jesus Christ; that we might receive the promise of the Spirit through faith."

All of this based on faith. It's not earned but given. We only need to believe, and that is faith.

Believing, you receive.

Kneeling, you are blessed.

And as Abraham, you are blessed to be a blessing.

Your words of blessing are life-giving. Knowing this God-given part of the power of how He created you is of tremendous purpose that adds so much fullness to your own life. It can impact everything around you to His glory! We pray it, "Your Kingdom come, Your will be done." Blessings are of the Kingdom. When we see them on earth as they are in heaven, our joy and praise is for the One Who gave us our very breath and every blessing.

CHAPTER FIFTEEN
PRAISING

HALLELU-YAH!

Praise is a way of using our breath that is extraordinary. It is a form of worship and it is the ultimate expression of worship that we can breathe out.

> *"Let everything that has breath praise the LORD."*
> *(Psalm 150:6)*

Your placement of being called and chosen for this time in the world matters, and so does your praise and worship.

The definition of "praise" in the Free Dictionary of Farlex reads:

---

n. 1. Expression of approval, commendation, or admiration.
2. The extolling or exaltation of a deity, ruler, or hero.
3. Archaic A reason for praise; merit.

tr.v. praised, prais·ing, prais·es:
1. To express warm approbation of, commendation for, or admiration for.
2. To extol or exalt; worship.

The word "hallelujah" is universally known. It is a word proclaimed in joy, gratitude, and worship. The root word *halal* (or spelled hillul or hallel) is for praise, which means, "to be clear, to shine, boast, rave, celebrate, show, and be clamorously foolish."

This is a breakdown of the word "hallelujah" from Strong's Concordance:

1974. הִלּוּלִים (hillul) -- a rejoicing, praise... לְהַלְלוּהָ rejoicing, praise: ... Hebrew). merry, praise. 1984b. halal -- to be boastful, to praise...

3050. יָהּ (Yah) -- the name of the God of Israel... Elsewhere יָהּ is used only in late Psalms, especially in the Hallels.

---

1 Shout with joy to YHVH, all the earth!
2 Worship YHVH with gladness.
Come before him, singing with joy.
3 Acknowledge that YHVH is God!
He made us, and we are his.
We are his people, the sheep of his pasture.
4 Enter his gates with thanksgiving;
go into his courts with praise.
Give thanks to him and praise his name.
5 For YHVH is good.
His unfailing love continues forever,
and his faithfulness continues to each generation.
(Psalm 100)

The word *yadah* is a Hebrew verb with the root meaning, "the extended hand, to throw out the hand, therefore to worship with extended hand." According to the lexicon, the opposite meaning is "to bemoan, the wringing of the hands."

The physical raising of hands in praise is the opposite of wringing our hands.

When we raise our hands, we let go of everything else and reach to God.

People readily raise their hands in the air as they celebrate. When someone makes a goal or scores in a sports game, people jump up and raise their hands for joy.

We do it without even thinking. When we are nervous about a game, worried, and fear a loss, we go into the handwringing. These are two examples of ways we react. We react like this in emotional and spiritual ways, too.

People have often restricted themselves from showing the joy and celebration of gratitude and thankfulness and worship to God by not raising their hands. This isn't natural, and for whatever reason, people have brought in restrictive and confining behavior into a lot of church settings.

Some people are self-conscious in expressing themselves by raising their hands. However, when you put your focus on YHVH and not on yourself or those around you, it becomes easier to raise your hand to Him.

God-consciousness delivers boldness without fear.

The intentional decision to praise and raise your hands to the Creator also keeps you from doing the opposite: bemoaning or wringing your hands. When you are troubled, try praising and worshiping God.

That extended hand and worship as you focus on the Creator makes concerns fall away, and a peace comes that is unexplainable. You are opening up your body and mind and spirit to connecting with God as you speak out or sing praises to Him.

Towdah comes from the same principle root word as *yadah*, but it is used more specifically. *Towdah* literally means, "an extension of the hand in adoration, avowal, or acceptance." (Towdah Radio.com; The Meaning of Towdah)

By way of application, in the Psalms and elsewhere it is used for thanking God for "things not yet received" as well as things already at hand. (*Ancient Hebrew Lexicon of the Bible.* Jeff Benner)

This is a large expression of faith. In those moments, God moves.

2 Chronicles 20 is a great example of this, and it is one of my favorite passages in the Bible. It helped me move into allowing God to do some life-changing work.

King Jehosophat and the people of Judah were surrounded by armies of their enemies. In all practical thought, they knew they could not win against them without the help of YHVH.

So they cried out to YHVH, reminding Him of the inheritance He had originally given and promised. They fasted and prayed with their faces to the ground. The men, women, and children all joined in together to seek YHVH's help.

The Holy Spirit came upon one of them, and he began to prophecy and speak. He told them to go out to the battle and stand there. They did not need to fight or lift a finger, but that the battle belonged to YHVH and He was going to deliver them.

With that, they got up the next morning, and King Jehosophat called them to believe in YHVH their God and they will succeed. He even appointed singers and people to praise YHVH that walked in front. This is what they sang and praised in verse 21: "Give thanks to YHVH, for his steadfast love endures forever."

And then in verse 22... "And when they began to sing and praise, YHVH set an ambush against the men of Ammon, Moab, and Mount Seir, who had come against Judah, so that they were routed."

This was when and where YHVH's ambush took place. It happened at the time of their praise and singing. They did not fear; rather they focused on Him, believed in Him, and worshiped Him. In that fullness of trust, faith, adoration, rest, and praises, His presence powerfully defeated the enemy.

Scripture says in Psalm 22:3 that YHVH inhabits and is enthroned on the praises of Israel/His people. His power, holiness, and the sheer magnitude of His holy presence dwell amid the praises. The Enemy is defeated in that powerful presence, and fear has no place in the midst of God-conscious adoration and focus.

When I began to praise God and worship Him more than just praying and begging for help, I began to sense His presence more. At first, my singing and praise proved difficult for me as I tried to sing past the lump in my throat and my broken heart. All I could sing was, "Holy, holy, holy."

But that is everything. He is, if one word were to describe Him, *holy*. So much is He, that it is the one word repeated three times in a row in Isaiah 6:3 and Revelation 4:8. I also see the use of "Holy" three times for each part of Himself revealed to us: Father, Son, and Holy Spirit. It is a trinity of holiness in the repetition of the word three times.

For Judah and King Jehosophat, God moved, and their enemies turned on themselves. Not a one of them survived, and the valley was full of the valuable spoils of their enemies. The people of Judah ran down and collected it all for themselves. There was so much, they were collecting for three days.

On the fourth day they assembled in the Valley of Beracah. You may recognize the pronunciation and another phonetic spelling of *Berakh* or Valley of Blessing.

Scripture says, "for there, they blessed YHVH." They returned to Jerusalem with joy because YHVH had caused them to rejoice over their enemies. 2 Chronicles 20:26

This is praise. When we praise, we begin to finally reach the place of rejoicing. Nothing else matters, only YHVH. They returned to Jerusalem with harps, lyres and trumpets.

Praising before God moves is shown in the word *towdah*. This example of King Jehosophat and Judah's praise is *towdah*. It is beautiful to me that the Hebrew have a word specifically for this kind of praise—a praise for things not yet received. This is fullness of faith and the knowledge of who He is while in complete relationship with Him.

Acts 16:16-40 shows a variety of situations that come about because of God's power through words, His name, and in worship and praise.

First, Paul and Silas were staying in Philippi and going down for prayer. A woman possessed with an evil spirit followed them and had been day after day. She was a fortune-teller. She followed them shouting that Paul and Silas were "servants of the Most High God." This was true; evil spirits recognize YHVH and those who serve Him.

It went on until Paul got so "exasperated" that he turned and commanded the demon to come out in the name of Yeshua the Christ. The Scripture says, "And instantly, it left her." By his words and the name of Yeshua, the demon had to leave.

The men that owned her and made money from her fortune telling were angry for the loss of their income and wealth and demanded that Paul and Silas be put in prison. The ensuing mob insisted they be jailed, and they severely beat and flogged Paul and Silas. They were considered so dangerous that the jailer put them in the inner dungeon where even their feet were bound.

Paul and Silas had a bad day, but it was for great purpose. They were doing good, going about their prayers, then they cast out a demon and all the bad happened to them. But their faith was in God, and they knew His goodness and kept their attention on Him no matter what had happened.

They weren't complaining to each other or to YHVH that they didn't deserve to be beaten and put in jail after all the good they had just done for Him. Rather, they kept in relationship with YHVH.

Around midnight, Scripture says, they were praying and singing hymns to YHVH.

Singing to God is praise and worship. All that they were—beaten, wounded, bound and in the deepest part of prison—was cast aside from their thoughts, and all that God is was their focus. The other prisoners listened to their prayers and songs, and suddenly the prison shook to its foundations. All the doors swung open, and all of the chains of *every* prisoner fell off.

This is another example of YHVH's power and movement in the midst of praise: The jailer was certain they had all escaped and was going to kill himself out of fear of the punishment coming for having lost all of the prisoners.

But Paul and Silas told him they were still there, and the jailer fell down before them trembling. He invited them into his home and washed their wounds, and Scripture says that everyone in the jailer's household believed and were baptized that night.

These results all started with prayer, a deliverance in Yeshua's name, prayer again, and then singing. YHVH freed many from the bondages not only of prison in the physical but also the prison and bondage of a dark life without Him.

Paul and Silas show that even in the worst of circumstances, He is worthy of our praise, and looking to Him in worship frees us from everything else. It also shows how one changed life can influence an entire household. God used the jailer's relationship with his household to bring more to Him. Our relationships matter.

What is interesting is that in the chapter before this happened, they were baptizing. After the event regarding the woman, the beating, getting thrown in jail, and being freed, it ends in baptism. His waters, life in baptism, and our praises, singing, and testimony are born on breaths of the water of life.

"Give thanks in all circumstances, for this is God's will for you in Christ Yeshua... (1 Thessalonians 5:18)

> "And give thanks for everything to God the Father in the name of our Lord Yeshua the Christ." (Ephesians 5:20)

An Old Testament example of being in a terrible place is found in Jonah 2. Jonah knew YHVH's will for him, but he tried to avoid it. In fact, Jonah 1:2 says, "But Jonah got up and went in the opposite direction to get away from Yahweh."

I get such a kick out of these things. People have always been people. We think we can do things our way, but when God has called us, we can either go peacefully or be brought to the place of peace the long way.

As Jonah is on the ship going the opposite way, the seas raged and a storm came. The sailors drew lots to see who it was that had riled up their god. The lot fell to Jonah, and they insisted on knowing his nationality and who his god was.

Jonah said he worshiped the God of Heaven that made the land and sea. They already knew he was running away from Yahweh. In verse 10, they groaned, "Oh, why did you do it?"

Jonah told them that if they threw him off the ship, it would all stop. The sailors first tried to row even harder to the shore, but it only got worse. They had been moved to speak to Yahweh themselves.

Verse 14 reads: "Then they cried to Creator Yahweh, Jonah's God. 'O Yahweh,' they pleaded, 'don't make us die for this man's sin. And don't hold us responsible for his death. O Yahweh, you have sent this storm upon him for your own good reasons.'"

That's a lot of instant knowledge.

They recognized Yahweh, they feared His ability at being responsible for their life, they recognized sin in disobedience, and they knew that the penalty for another's death was serious. But they also knew the storm was upon them because Jonah was with them, so they laid it all out before Yahweh. Then they picked Jonah up and tossed him into the sea.

Talk about a baptism.

Jonah had admitted his wrong-doing and released himself to Yahweh. He literally was going to die to himself. In witness of the power of God, as soon as Jonah was in the water, the sea calmed and the storm stopped. The sailors were awestruck at the Creator Yahweh's great power, and they offered Him a sacrifice and vowed to follow Him.

Because of where Jonah was at the time, Yahweh/YHVH used his relationship, time, and place to bring the sailors to Himself. But Yahweh wasn't done.

It says in verse 17, "Now Yahweh had arranged for a great fish to swallow Jonah. And Jonah was inside the fish for three days and three nights."

I have heard people say that this is just a story. It couldn't have happened. But I have seen documentaries showing fish with abnormally large cavities capable of maintaining a large amount of air inside.

All things are possible with Yahweh.

Not only is this not "just a story" but Yeshua also used this example of Jonah in the fish for three days in describing His own upcoming death-and-resurrection timeframe. What was happening had a prophetic purpose that came hundreds of years later for Yeshua to use.

Where this draws into praise in all circumstances is Jonah 2:9: "But I will offer sacrifices to you with songs of praise, and I will fulfill my vows. For my salvation comes from Yahweh alone."

Praise, in the most difficult of times, is sacrificial. Jonah is inside a fish!

It means sacrificing yourself and troubles—in other words, not letting it be about you but instead glorifying God for what He has given us: salvation, life, and all things good in His Holy, sovereign, splendor. This is sacrificial praise.

All sacrifice is letting go of our good for another's. Our good always pales by comparison to Yahweh's good.

Jonah had gone through a long prayer in chapter two, but as he turned it into the words of sacrificial praise, it reads in verse 10: "Then Yahweh ordered the fish to spit Jonah out onto the beach."

Jonah was *immediately* freed when he praised. I wonder how many laps the fish had to go back and forth along the shore until Jonah finally reached the point of praising?

God is merciful even in our disobedience. He will give us more mercy or chances to try again. Chapter 3 says that God then asked Jonah a second time to, "Get up and go to the great city of Nineveh." Verse 3 says, "This time Jonah obeyed and went."

Jonah's life was changed. He was beginning a life of prophet as he spoke for God to the people of Nineveh.

"Through Yeshua, therefore, let us continually offer to God a sacrifice of praise—the fruit of lips that confess his name. 16And do not forget to do good and to share with others, for with such sacrifices God is pleased." (Hebrews 13:15-16)

The book of Psalms is filled with praises or *hallels*. Remember, *hallel* is a Hebrew word for "praise" like in "Hallelujah." It was part of David's heart.

He would begin in prayer (or sometimes rants), then he would turn his thoughts back onto the goodness of Yahweh, and he would be calm, peace-filled, and secure. He worked his heart back to hope, and Yahweh poured it into him through His love.

Our human nature could do better to be more conditioned to praise first. It would avoid a whole lot of upset.

My cousin once told me a story about her mom, my aunt. She said her mom put praise into practice, and sometimes it would drive my cousin crazy. She said she would misplace her purse, and her mom would say, "Have you praised God for it yet?"

My aunt really lives it, and her life shows it. She walks in nearly continuous joy, peace, and blessing. She confesses the beauty and Yahweh's grace that comes when she praises in all circumstances. My cousin said there were times where she would think to herself, "All I want to do is find my purse!"

～

We have learned much about some of the people that worked at the Twin Towers in NYC. In some cases, their life troubles on the morning of 9/11 as they tried to get to work were the very things that saved their lives. Some had transportation problems and hadn't made it into work. Someone else had a sick child and had to stay home, and so on.

In the moment, it seemed like a nuisance and a difficulty. But they confessed with enormous gratitude that it was what had saved them. We don't always know how things that appear bad may be benefiting us in another way. Yahweh is worthy of our praise.

～

My real estate business had slowed up a lot. I have to confess that I complained and prayed and didn't do much praising. But now I can see that it allowed me to focus on God's Word and to see the things He had to show me regarding this message. It also allowed me more time to write.

I can praise Him for it now, and I praise Him for what I learned from Him in that time. There is purpose, and He allows it.

Singing is praising. It takes a lot to sing to Yahweh when we don't feel like it. It can be done in joy very easily. When it is done in difficulty, it is sacrifice.

Music and song is a gift from Him to us. It can pull our thoughts back to Him, and some of my most profoundly moving times in connecting with Yahweh have happened through music and song. Sometimes we lose ourselves in the music, and that's where our focus can fully shift to God.

Full-out worship in singing makes us forget about ourselves, and we become focused on YHVH, the music, and our words to Him.

Sometimes people start tapping or swaying or dancing as they put themselves into the music. Tiny children often bounce and move to music as it fills their whole body.

David praised YHVH and danced in complete focus on Him. David's thoughts were not at all on himself. The Ark of the Covenant was being delivered back to Bethlehem, and David was bringing it there amid rejoicing and worship. Every six steps they stopped and made a burnt sacrifice to YHVH. They must have grown happier and happier with every stop.

David's complete abandon, joy, and focus solely on YHVH manifested in a carelessness in the way he appeared. He wore only a linen ephod, and we hear how his wife, Michal, was disgusted at others seeing him. She was focused on herself and of what people thought of her husband, not on YHVH. She even used the cruelty of sarcasm as she addressed him.

Wearing a linen ephod, David was dancing before the Lord with all his might, 15 while he and all Israel were bringing up the ark of YHVH/Yahweh with shouts and the sound of trumpets.

> 14 And David danced before the LORD with all his might; and David was girded with a linen ephod. 15 So David and all the house of Israel brought up the ark of the LORD with shouting, and with the sound of the trumpet.
>
> 16 And it was so, as the ark of the LORD came into the city of David, that Michal the daughter of Saul looked out at the window, and saw king David leaping and dancing before the LORD; and she despised him in her heart.
>
> 17 And they brought in the ark of the LORD, and set it in its place, in the midst of the tent that David had pitched for it: and David offered burnt offerings and peace offerings before the LORD. 18 And when David had made an end of offering the burnt offering and the peace offerings, he blessed the people in the name of the LORD of hosts. 19 And he dealt among all the

> people, even among the whole multitude of Israel, both to men and women, to every one a cake of bread, and a portion of flesh, and a cake of raisins. So all the people departed every one to his house.
>
> 20 Then David returned to bless his household. And Michal the daughter of Saul came out to meet David, and said, How glorious was the king of Israel today, who uncovered himself today in the eyes of the handmaids of his servants, as one of the vain fellows shamelessly uncovereth himself!
>
> 21 And David said unto Michal, It was before the LORD, which chose me above thy father, and above all his house, to appoint me prince over the people of the LORD, over Israel: therefore will I play before the LORD. 22 And I will be yet more vile than thus, and will be base in mine own sight: but of the handmaids which thou hast spoken of, of them shall I be had in honour. 23 And Michal the daughter of Saul had no child unto the day of her death. (2 Samuel 6:14-23)

Verse 23 indicates that this rift most likely kept David from desiring her anymore, and it reads that she despised David in her heart. Yahweh may also have stopped her ability to bear children as she spoke such contempt. David had come to bless his household, and the blessing after this exchange probably did not take place for her as his devotion was always to God first.

As a musician, David would have likely been all the more moved in worship and praise by music. There are some amazing things in music theory. The notes repeat every eight notes, either going an octave higher or lower.

Look at the word "octave." *Oct* is a Greek root word for "eight," like in an octagon (an eight-sided object). And again, eight marks the start of new beginning in Hebrew. Music can bring that kind of life and energy by the principles of following this design.

We remember songs and lyrics that we heard even years ago. The memory of certain songs trigger times and places from years gone by. Often, couples will choose a song that represents them and their courtship.

Music is also universal. Our gift to make music and sing music and enjoy music is a pleasure from the Creator and one that we can give back in praise and worship. No wonder why music is brought into praise, it is designed in a way that few have noticed. It has the potential of life and new beginnings when used in praise to God. It draws us into an ultimate freedom when we release ourselves into the majesty and presence of YHVH. He moves us from the inside out.

CHAPTER SIXTEEN
DESIGN

The more I paid attention to patterns in nature and living things, I saw perfection. Only God could have designed such perfection over and over again. The revelation of design throughout creation is inescapable in life. For design, a Designer is inherent. Eight notes in music and then a repeat. In science, we follow the trails of design and those that lead to origin.

Science continuously seeks out origin. Origin is part of the word "originator" or the word "original," as in the one that was first before a duplicate or copy was made. Everything we have ever made has come by design. Some things may not have occurred as we planned, but some sort of intentionality in another direction brought forth the unplanned result.

I have heard people say that man, Earth, and life came about by "dumb luck." Is "dumb" that lucky? If we believe it is dumb luck, it is a belief, nonetheless. One's belief either goes to dumb luck instead of the Creator/YHVH. I know which I would rather believe in.

There is more design in our words and sound. The intricacy of sound in its form of waves likens to water. Sound has sound *waves*. Our words create sound waves. One does not worship the waves, the water, the sound, or energy but rather the One who created and designed it all.

Seismographs show the *waves* captured by the needle movements from the kinetic energy of movement from our Earth. There are light *waves* and electromagnetic *waves*. Waves are everywhere in our natural world.

When we see the order of these waves, the common attributes of behavior to consistently associate "waves" with these various forms of energy, there is design. If there is a design, there is a designer. The designer is the originator. This is too perfect to be random and luck. We have a Creator to praise!

When we study those who create, we can see many masterpieces by various artists. You can become familiar with a style of the particular artist. You can recognize their work. It holds true for authors and their work, filmmakers, jewelers, architects, and musicians. If you study art, you can recognize a Monet, a Van Gogh, a Remington or a Picasso.

When we look at the natural and the style in types of energy, they all emit waves, too. In living things like trees, plants, animals, fish, birds, and people, one of the common elements we share is veining and cells. It's part of the design of much of life.

Planets and solar systems have orbits. Atoms also orbit. From the minute to the large, there is a common design... there is a Designer imprint.

Sometimes the term "evolution" is used to try to distant itself from a Creator, but there is always an origin. We cannot escape a source or origin even in evolution. As I looked at dinosaur bones with my young son in the science museum loaded with written theories of evolution, he said, "But a tooth is a tooth."

> "Yes, they knew God, but they wouldn't worship him as God or even give him thanks. And they began to think up foolish ideas of what God was like. As a result, their minds became dark and confused..." (Romans 1:21)

Our words and our singing come from a fullness of our being (*nephesh*) and life (*chai/khai*). It is unique to us by our breath and voice and the song or words we say. Singing can share a fullness of vulnerability, of joy, or of sorrow.

The heights and depths of emotion are often made known to a greater extent in song as our voices raise waves unseen, but heard.

Singing to God is not one-sided. "The LORD your God is in your midst, a mighty one who will save; he will rejoice over you with gladness; he will quiet you by his love; he will exult over you with loud singing." (Zephaniah 3:17)

Our Lord sings over us with rejoicing, gladness, and love. This is where the connection of our own praise meets His, and the power of that unity ignites great things on Earth and in Heaven.

"Yet you are holy, enthroned on the praises of Israel." (Psalm 22:3)

Music, singing, and blessing were a large part of the Hebrew people and their culture. I recently watched a PBS documentary called, *Broadway Musicals: A Jewish Legacy*. It told of all of the Jewish people who wrote America's Broadway musicals and how these songs were part of American identity in way of song, music, theater, and production.

The industry exploded as these songs captivated people. Composers like Irving Berlin, Jerome Kern, George and Ira Gershwin, Lorenz Hart, Richard Rodgers, Oscar Hammerstein II, Kurt Weill, Sheldon Harnick, Jerry Bock, Leonard Bernstein, Stephen Sondheim, Stephen Schwartz, Jule Styne, and others enriched us in waves of song and musicals.

What I didn't know until watching this documentary was that many of their songs had the underlying melody of Jewish songs and blessings. Over and over again, they played some that were not so obvious and others that were very obvious.

A stand-out to me was the song *God Bless America* by Irving Berlin. He wrote it as a blessing and a prayer. He never wanted to make a penny from it, and the truth to that was in his precise collection of royalties for his other music and none from this song.

Music, lyrics, worship, and praise are powerful connectors to Yahweh. In all of Creation, there is much to be thankful for and to praise Him for and to be in awe of His Holiness. He reveals His heart through His love for us, the life given from the creation of Mother Earth, and His desire to save us from condemnation of sin by His coming as Christ Yeshua.

Being "God as man" is unfathomable humility. Pouring out His own blood and dying for our sins in order to be in full relationship with Him forever is the greatest act imaginable. Because of His time in a physical body on earth, we get to know what it is like to walk in relationship with Him now in Spirit. We are able to live in relationship with Him now on earth through His Spirit.

This is a holy love. You are created because of His love for you and His love for the world He created. He made ways to be in relationship with you in power through your faith.

CHAPTER SEVENTEEN
HORNS OF PRAISE, POWER, AND FAITH

Have you ever blown a horn? After a while, it gets full of saliva from being blown. Or have you blown up a balloon and let the air out to zip around the room? After a while, it shoots out spit with the air.

If you have ever played a wind or brass instrument or tried blowing into one, you can recall the amount of effort it took to produce a sound. You had to take a large breath and exert it to a great extent, like blowing up a balloon the first time.

Some of us maybe even remember the spit-valve on our instrument as the moisture from your breath poured through and needed to be released, and it dripped onto the floor. Or at the least, you may remember cleaning the instrument after having played it a while, in order to dry it out and pack it up again.

Our breath and water is part of making a horn make sound.

The blowing of a horn or Shofar is mentioned in the Bible eighty-eight times.

Blowing a shofar horn is associated with the power of Yahweh or often in the act of faith by His people. A shofar, or sometimes called a trumpet in the Bible, is made out of a ram's horn.

Look at 2 Samuel 6:14-15: "Wearing a linen ephod, David was dancing before Yahweh with all his might, 15 while he and all Israel were bringing up the ark of YHVH with shouts and the sound of trumpets."

That reference to trumpets and shouting in Hebrew is the word *teruah*.

Shouts come with great force of breath, and so does the blowing of horns.

Notice these verses and their association with strong faith and the power of YHVH:

"And he has raised up for his people a horn, the praise of all his faithful servants, of Israel, the people close to his heart. Praise Yahweh/YHVH..." (Psalm 148:14)

"On the morning of the third day there was thunder and lightning, with a thick cloud over the mountain, and a very loud trumpet blast, so that everyone in the camp trembled." (Exodus 19:16)

"And when the voice of the trumpet sounded long, and grew louder and louder, Moses spoke, and God answered him in thunder" (Exodus 19:19)

"Then the LORD will appear over them, And His arrow will go forth like lightning; And the Lord GOD will blow the trumpet, And will march..." (Zechariah 9:14 NKJ)

Can you even imagine the sound of God blowing a trumpet and the power and Holiness behind it? I don't know that our earthly bodies could survive it. "And he will send his angels with a great sound of a trumpet, and they will gather his elect from the four winds, from one end of heaven to the other." (Matthew 24:31 NKJ)

I'm not sure what the four horns on the brazen altar really signify, but I do think of them as they were to be on the four corners of the altar in Exodus 27:2. It may be another link of physical to spiritual between the Old and New Testament. Possibly the four winds?

> "It will happen in a moment, in the blink of an eye, when the last trumpet is blown. For when the trumpet sounds, those who have died will be raised to live forever. And we who are living will also be transformed." (1 Corinthians 15:52 NLT)

Revelations 8-10 goes over the final days of Earth and the seven angels with the seven trumpets.

At multiple times, God had the trumpets blown. He also shows where He called people to blow trumpets out of faith and trust, and in doing so, by the exertion of their breath, God proved faithful and powerful.

The walls of Jericho fell down at the command of YHVH, using nothing more than the breath of His people and walking in obedience. He told them to blow the ram's horn (shofar). He commanded that seven priests to blow the ram's horn and it will be a signal to shout.

> Now Jericho was shut up inside and outside because of the people of Israel. None went out, and none came in. 2 And Yahweh said to Joshua, "See, I have given Jericho into your hand, with its king and mighty men of valor. 3 You shall march around the city, all the men of war going around the city once. Thus shall you do for six days. 4 Seven priests shall bear seven trumpets of rams' horns before the ark. On the seventh day you shall march around the city seven times, and the priests shall blow the trumpets. 5 And when they make a long blast with the ram's horn, when you hear the sound of the trumpet, then all the people shall shout with a great shout, and the wall of the

city will fall down flat, and the people shall go up, everyone straight before him." (Joshua 6:1-5)

Note that in Hebrew the word *teruah* here translates to "shout with a great shout."

As it reads farther down in Joshua, the people did these things, and the walls that had fortified the city came down, leading to Yahweh's destruction of their enemies. Yet one was saved, along with her household, for being a friend to Israel and helping to hide them and keep them safe.

She was Rahab, a prostituted woman of Jericho, and Yahweh saw in His mercy to set her free. Later, Yahweh brought Yeshua/Jesus through her lineage. Her story in this is also the story of Yahweh's love for those in bondage and oppression.

I found Joshua 6:10 interesting. It emphasizes the absolute absence of their words in this act except for when it is time to shout: "But Joshua commanded the people, 'You shall not shout or make your voice heard, neither shall any word go out of your mouth, until the day I tell you to shout. Then you shall shout.'"

This seems to further emphasize the power of which the spoken words can help or harm. No idle word was said, and no form of doubt or disbelief could have been shared. No pride uttered, no fear spoken. The only sounds first heard were the trumpet blasts of the priests—the breath of those who walk most closely with Yahweh.

The message of Gideon in Judges 6-7 takes him from coward to bold warrior. Yahweh saw Gideon as courageous despite the way Gideon viewed himself. Yahweh slowly and patiently walked Gideon step-by-step from doubt and cowardice to a place of bold obedience in courageous faith.

Gideon didn't respond to YHVH's encouraging words at first.

People can speak well of us, but we have to receive them in order for them to take hold.

Gideon didn't even come close to receiving it. He responded in bitter doubt saying, "Well, if Yahweh is with us, why did all of this happen to us?" He continued his defiance by asking, "Where are His deeds? Where are the great things that our Father's told us about Him? Why has He forsaken us?"

Scripture says that Yahweh turned to him and said, "Go in this might of yours and deliver Israel out of the hand of the Midian. Do I not send you?"

Gideon realized that Yahweh was not backing down. Then Gideon started to list reasons why he was not capable of what he was being told to do. He went down the chain of weakness, saying, "Am I not from the weakest clan of all and am I not the least of my Father's household?"

YHVH responded and said, "But I will go with you and you will strike the Midianites as if one man." Yahweh had shrunk the strength of the Midians to be equal to only one man as He gave Gideon strength by being in relationship with Him.

Yahweh told Gideon to tear down his Father's altar to Baal. YHVH had a plan in this. Gideon obeyed, but he still had fear. ...But because he was too afraid of his family and the men of the town to do it by day, he did it by night. (Judges 6:27)

Gideon's willingness to obey was greater than being stopped by his fear. He did it while scared.

These things helped build Gideon's faith as he obeyed YHVH, and YHVH kept him safe.

But Gideon continued to doubt and asked YHVH for assurance. "If I have found favor with You," he says, "then prove it." Gideon laid out the terms. As Gideon saw YHVH'S response to his requests, it grew Gideon's faith to believe in what YHVH was doing, and their relationship grew.

But YHVH also made sure that Gideon was fully dependent on HIM. YHVH whittled down Gideon's army that had joined to fight the

Midians down to 300 men. Gideon was unnerved, and YHVH continued His mercy for Gideon.

YHVH instructed Gideon, and then Gideon instructed his men. He told them to each take a clay jar and place a lighted torch inside of the jar. They were each to take a trumpet, too.

> And they blew the trumpets and smashed the jars that were in their hands. 20 Then the three companies blew the trumpets and broke the jars. They held in their left hands the torches, and in their right hands the trumpets to blow. And they cried out, "A sword for YHVH and for Gideon!" (Judges 7:19-20)

These are the acts of powerful faith! Again, the symbolism of the clay jars references us: "But we have this treasure in jars of clay, to show that the surpassing power belongs to God/YHVH and not to us." (2 Corinthians 4:7)

Also, the torch was kept inside of them, and then the clay jars were broken (self) and the light shown. In a way, Gideon was like this. He believed in YHVH, but he wasn't fully living in His will, to the point of letting his own life be a light to others.

YHVH brought him forward step-by-step to be confident in Him and a leader by believing His Words. Gideon's self-centered concerns, worries, and doubts yielded to God's faithful proof in not forsaking Him.

Gideon's faith became so strong that it made his army's faith and obedience strong. They faced an enemy as many as the grains of sand on the shore, exposed themselves of where they were with the torch light, and with all the breath that they had, they blasted their trumpets of faith and proclaimed in a great shout, "A sword for YHVH!"

This is one of my most favorite examples of breath in a powerful exertion of faith. It isn't the mumble of a half-conscious, repetitive prayer but rather a blast of whole-hearted faith of who YHVH is and what He will do and the knowing that His promises are kept. They had the victory through Him.

Scripture goes to say that the Midianite army fled. "When they blew the 300 trumpets, YHVH set every man's sword against his comrade and against all the army." (Judges 7:22)

The enemy/Midianites turned on their friends and their own army. It happened not when Gideon and his men smashed the jars, not when they lifted the torches or when they shouted, but after all of that, when they blew the trumpets.

Remember that YHVH called Gideon, "O mighty man of valor" *while* Gideon was hiding from the Midianites? Valor means "courage in the face of danger," according to Merriam Dictionary.

YHVH saw Gideon the way he was in Him. He ignored Gideon's view of himself and stripped it away until all Gideon looked to and saw was YHVH. His whole breath blasted out his faith through the trumpet.

Faith is provided by YHVH. He leads us gently there. He proves Himself again and again, and He reveals more of Himself to grow our relationship in trust, love, strength, and His power. He is patient with us, He is merciful with us, and He wants us to know Him in peace and trust and love. He is worthy of our praise, and He provides for our faith.

> Looking to Yeshua/Jesus the author and finisher of our faith; who for the joy that was set before him endured the cross, despising the shame, and is set down at the right hand of the throne of God. 3For consider him that endured such contradiction of sinners against himself, lest you be wearied and faint in your minds. (Hebrews 12:2-3)

---

29 By faith the people crossed the Red Sea as on dry land, but the Egyptians, when they attempted to do the same, were drowned. 30 By faith the walls of Jericho fell down after they had been encircled for seven days. 31 By faith Rahab the prostitute did not perish with those who were disobedient, because she had given a friendly welcome to the spies.

32 And what more shall I say? For time would fail me to tell of Gideon, Barak, Samson, Jephthah, of David and Samuel and the prophets— 33 who through faith conquered kingdoms, enforced justice, obtained promises, stopped the mouths of lions, 34 quenched the power of fire, escaped the edge of the sword, were made strong out of weakness, became mighty in war, put foreign armies to flight. 35 Women received back their dead by resurrection. Some were tortured, refusing to accept release, so that they might rise again to a better life. 36 Others suffered mocking and flogging, and even chains and imprisonment. 37 They were stoned, they were sawn in two, they were killed with the sword. They went about in skins of sheep and goats, destitute, afflicted, mistreated— 38 of whom the world was not worthy—wandering about in deserts and mountains, and in dens and caves of the earth.

39 And all these, though commended through their faith, did not receive what was promised, 40 since God had provided something better for us, that apart from us they should not be made perfect. (Hebrews 11:29-40)

To reach the point to have a heart of gratitude in order to praise means something. It means you have reached a coming of faith. Yahweh made *Himself* known. Noticing Him, believing Him, trusting Him, and loving Him as the Giver of all that you have—life—is worth our constant praise to Him.

Holy, Holy, Holy is Yahweh God Almighty.

There is a Hebrew festival called Rosh Hashana, or the Feast of Trumpets. In Hebrew, it is called *Yom Teruah*. Recognize the word *teruah*? YHVH ordained a festival to be celebrated every year. It matters to Him. It is the breath of bold faith, celebration, and praise. It is worship of Him and His power, encompassed in His power.

In the book of Ezra, when the Israelites had been freed from Babylon and began building their temple again, they shouted in great joy to Yahweh and the place of His presence. Again, in this passage, the shout in Hebrew is the word *teruah*.

> "Speak to the sons of Israel, saying, 'In the seventh month on the first of the month you shall have a rest, a reminder by blowing of trumpets, a holy convocation.'" (Leviticus 23:24 NASB)

Teruah is also the blowing of trumpets for the celebration of the Day of Atonement in the year of Jubilee.

> "Count off seven sabbath years—seven times seven years—so that the seven sabbath years amount to a period of forty-nine years. 9Then have the trumpet sounded everywhere on the tenth day of the seventh month; on the Day of Atonement sound the trumpet throughout your land. 10Consecrate the fiftieth year and proclaim liberty throughout the land to all its inhabitants. It shall be a jubilee for you; each of you is to return to your family property and to your own clan." (Leviticus 25:8-10 NIV)
>
> "It will happen in a moment, in the blink of an eye, when the last trumpet is blown. For when the trumpet sounds, those

who have died will be raised to live forever. And we who are living will also be transformed." (1 Corinthians 15:52)

It is in the breath that life comes forth in resurrection and in spirit. The glory of the King is sounded in triumphant victory and those who held Him to be faithful will see the glory of the King. From His throne flows a pure river of water of life... Rev. 22:1 Believers, there is reason to celebrate! There is life eternal within you, proclaim His Majesty and His victory!

CHAPTER EIGHTEEN
SPIRIT AND LIFE

Like the repetitive lapping of the ocean's waters against the shore or in grand, thunderous waves, the Lord repetitively moves in strength, or in gentle grace. He speaks or makes lives new around water. The fullness of this still holds mystery to me, but we have been led to recognize it now.

It is in places in the Word and more that we have yet to discover. As much as I thought I knew what would be in this writing from the beginning, much more has come that I had not seen until now.

> Then I, Daniel, looked, and behold, two others stood, one on this bank of the stream and one on that bank of the stream. 6And someone said to the man clothed in linen, who was above the waters of the stream "How long shall it be till the end of these wonders?" 7And I heard the man clothed in linen, who was above the waters of the stream; he raised his right hand and his left hand toward heaven and swore by him who lives forever that it would be for a time, times, and half a time, and that when the shattering of the power of the holy people comes to an end all these things would be finished. (Daniel 12:5-7 5)

I believe with all of my heart that the man clothed in linen who was above the waters was Yeshua/Jesus.

In Matthew 14:25, Yeshua is walking on the water, and it says that He came to the disciples who are on a boat. After having spent time in relationship with His disciples, Peter now knows Yeshua, but wants to be sure it is Him and desires to walk on the water and join Him. This is a powerful scene when you recognize the relationship that had formed between Peter and His Savior. Peter still lost site for a moment, but Yeshua reached out His hand and drew Peter back up.

Another life-changing place at the waters is found in the lives of both Elijah and Elisha in 2 Kings 2:6-15. Yahweh is going to take Elijah to be with Him, and this is one of the few places in Scripture of a man being taken without a physical death.

---

6 Then Elijah said to Elisha, "Stay here, for YHVH has told me to go to the Jordan River."

But again Elisha replied, "As surely as Yahweh lives and you yourself live, I will never leave you." So they went on together.

7 Fifty men from the group of prophets also went and watched from a distance as Elijah and Elisha stopped beside the Jordan River. 8 Then Elijah folded his cloak together and struck the water with it. The river divided, and the two of them went across on dry ground!

9 When they came to the other side, Elijah said to Elisha, "Tell me what I can do for you before I am taken away."

And Elisha replied, "Please let me inherit a double share of your spirit and become your successor."

10 "You have asked a difficult thing," Elijah replied. "If you see me when I am taken from you, then you will get your request. But if not, then you won't."

11 As they were walking along and talking, suddenly a chariot

of fire appeared, drawn by horses of fire. It drove between the two men, separating them, and Elijah was carried by a whirlwind into heaven. 12 Elisha saw it and cried out, "My father! My father! I see the chariots and charioteers of Israel!" And as they disappeared from sight, Elisha tore his clothes in distress.

13 Elisha picked up Elijah's cloak, which had fallen when he was taken up. Then Elisha returned to the bank of the Jordan River. 14 He struck the water with Elijah's cloak and cried out, "Where is the YHVH, the God of Elijah?" Then the river divided, and Elisha went across.

15 When the group of prophets from Jericho saw from a distance what happened, they exclaimed, "Elijah's spirit rests upon Elisha!" And they went to meet him and bowed to the ground before him.

YHVH continued to do life things around water. When Yeshua began His ministry, He first was baptized, then He was led to the desert and tempted by the Devil. The desert had no water, no evidence of the Father except in Christ Himself and the angels that were sent to strengthen Him after His ordeal.

What follows the time in the desert is found in Matthew 4:18. One day, Yeshua was walking the shore of the Sea of Galilee (which is also called the Lake of Gennesaret.) He went to the beautiful, freshwater Sea of Galilee and there, from the waters, He drew out His first two disciples.

They had been fishing, likely with nets while standing in the water, because the next two disciples He calls that also come from the Sea of Galilee are stated to come off of boats. Jesus' first followers are chosen from the waters and are called, "Fishers of Men."

They are men called out of the waters of His Spirit and grace. They were not priests in the priestly order, but men given grace through the love of Jesus.

The Sea of Galilee is fed by the Jordan River and by many springs beneath it. It is a fertile and beautiful place, and it is the area that Abraham received as second choice after his Nephew Lot had first choice of the land he would inhabit.

"Gennesaret" means "harp," but upon looking at the satellite image of Lake Gennesaret or Sea of Galilee, I was struck at the resemblance it also has to the human heart. This body of water, the lowest below sea-level that is made of freshwater, is the heart of the people and places of the Bible.

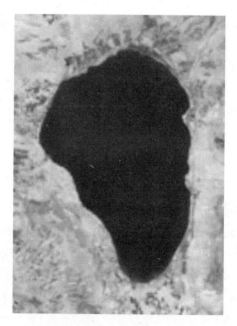

Source: NASA Satellite Image

The Sea of Galilee flows again into the Jordan River and into the Dead Sea. The Dead Sea is the lowest below sea-level of all bodies of water on earth. This was the land chosen as the best pick/first-pick by Lot when Abraham allowed him to choose first.

The land and cities flourished at one time around this area, teeming with life, water, and fertile land. The city of Sodom was situated here. An archaeological find was recently made identifying the city of Sodom. (*Discovering the City of Sodom: The Fascinating True Account of the Discovery of the Old Testament's Most Infamous City*, by Dr. Steven Collins and Dr. Latayne C. Scott) It was this city that desecrated the holiness of YHVH as found in Genesis 18.

YHVH had said He would destroy it, but Abraham pled with YHVH that if he found fifty righteous people, would He spare it?

YHVH said, "Yes."

Abraham became unsure if he could find that many. He asked YHVH that if he could find forty-five, would He spare it?

Again, YHVH replied, "Yes."

Then Abraham, worked his way down to forty, then thirty, then twenty people. Finally, Abraham asked if YHVH would spare it if he found ten righteous people.

In YHVH's incredible mercy and grace, He said he would spare it for ten. But not even ten righteous people were found.

God allowed Lot and some of his family to escape "because the compassion of YHVH was upon him." At that time, Scripture says that fire, sulfur, and brimstone from the sky overtook the city and land.

In scientific research of the Dead Sea and its geology, many scientists say that a sudden event happened where the waterbed dropped, that the types of minerals and salt occurred in a swift and sudden phenomenon, and to this day, it cannot support life. A life of desecration is no life.

The life is in YHVH, and He has shown it to us in all that lives and breathes around us and in His Word. We have a choice, to choose life or death, blessing or cursing. Christ came so that we may have life and have it abundantly, for He is "...the Way, the Truth and the Life, no one comes to the Father but through Me." (John 14:6)

"Whoever has the Son has life; whoever does not have the Son of God does not have life." (1 John 5:12)

Here is an amazing prophecy to come told from His Holy Spirit through the prophet Ezekiel. God's mercy and grace continues, even in what took place at the Dead Sea. The river of His temple will one day make it fresh and bring life. His Spirit will pour out, unstoppable and bring new Life.

---

1 Then he brought me back to the door of the temple, and behold, water was issuing from below the threshold of the temple toward the east (for the temple faced east). The water was flowing down from below the south end of the threshold of the temple, south of the altar. 2 Then he brought me out by way of the north gate and led me around on the outside to the outer gate that faces toward the east; and behold, the water was trickling out on the south side.

3 Going on eastward with a measuring line in his hand, the man measured a thousand cubits, and then led me through the water, and it was ankle-deep. 4 Again he measured a thousand, and led me through the water, and it was knee-deep. Again he measured a thousand, and led me through the water, and it was waist-deep. 5 Again he measured a thousand, and it was a river that I could not pass through, for the water had risen. It was deep enough to swim in, a river that could not be passed through. 6 And he said to me, "Son of man, have you seen this?"

Then he led me back to the bank of the river. 7 As I went back, I saw on the bank of the river very many trees on the one side and on the other. 8 And he said to me, "This water flows toward the eastern region and goes down into the Arabah, and enters the sea; when the water flows into the sea, the water will become fresh. ⁹ And wherever the river goes,ᵈ every living creature that swarms will live, and there will be very many fish. For this water goes there, that the waters of the seaᵉ may become fresh; so everything will live where the river goes. 10 Fishermen will stand beside the sea. From Engedi to Eneglaim it will be a place for the spreading of nets. Its fish will be of very many kinds, like the fish of the Great Sea.ᶠ 11 But its swamps and marshes will not become fresh; they are to be left for salt. 12 And on the banks, on both sides of the river, there will grow all kinds of trees for food. Their leaves will not wither, nor their fruit fail, but they will bear fresh fruit every month, because the water for them flows from the sanctuary. Their fruit will be for food, and their leaves for healing."

This is *huge*. The spiritual implication appears to be that those who were spiritually dead will receive the waters and Spirit of YHVH. His Words and truths and Spirit will pour fresh into them, and life will teem. They will live, and they will thrive.

Recall also Ezekiel's earlier vision of life being restored to the bones dead in the valley as he spoke YHVH's words over them and spoke to the winds and breath.

What is coming is likely to be the Word of YHVH and His revelation into the lives of men that had faded away and died in the valley spiritually, as well as a new life coming to the Dead Sea.

From the very beginning of Creation and the perfect Eden, YHVH prepared a place flowing with four rivers in Genesis 2:10-15.

The rivers were named Pishon, which means "Increase;" Gihon means "Bursting Forth;" the third river, Hiddekel (which is also the Tigris) means "Rapid;" and the fourth, Euphrates, means "Fruitfulness." (Strong's Concordance Hebrew Dictionary) From the beginning,

YHVH's desire through His rivers and waters have been Increase, Bursting Forth, Rapid, and Fruitful.

To living, *l'chaim*! *Chai* is the Hebrew word for "life." The "C" is hard and pronounced in the back of the throat as the "h" is exhaled on the breath. Its numeric value is the number eighteen.

Chai is eighteen in Hebrew numeral assignments.

The Hebrew word is written like this: חי

Hebrew people will give gifts in equivalent to the number eighteen when people marry, signifying a blessing for a good life. The *chai* symbol for the word "life" or "living" is popular in jewelry and medals for the Hebrew people. Life is revered. Sometimes the word is spelled in English as "hai." Notice the breath in the word as you say it.

My father is a physicist, and as I shared with him the revelation of water and life in YHVH's Word in the Bible and the association of the number eighteen with *Khayim/Chaim/Chai*, I was eager to remind him that the number eighteen had always been my favorite number since I was a little girl.

He got a smile on his face and said, "Lori, the number equivalent in chemistry for water is the number eighteen."

I screamed with joy!

Water is H^2O. H is for hydrogen, and hydrogen has the number equivalent of one. H is squared and equals *two* in water. O is for oxygen and has the number equivalent of sixteen. 2+16=18, and that is where water receives its numeric value chemically. Life!

The Gihon Spring in Jerusalem is the place where Solomon was anointed as king. (1 Kings 1:33-34) It leads to the Pool of Siloam, where Yeshua had the blind man wipe the mud from his eyes that Yeshua had placed on them (dirt of the earth mixed with the saliva/water of Yeshua's own mouth).

When the blind man washed his eyes in that pool of water that had come from the Spring of Gihon (bursting forth) he could see. Yeshua is giving us the vision today of Himself in the waters and the very essence of Him in us, for us, and life-giving in the physical and spiritual. Siloam means *sent*. Yeshua was sent as the reflection of YHVH incarnate.

In John 13, as Yeshua/Jesus knelt at the feet of His disciples and washed their feet, He knelt as servant to them. Peter wanted to be washed completely, all of himself, but Yeshua/Jesus said when you have had a bath, your whole body is clean and that he only needed his feet washed.

Feet are what come into contact with the world, the dust of the Earth. As we walk on our journey of life, we can become dirty by the dust of this Earth where we must walk.

Yeshua/Jesus' example was that those who teach also must serve. There is none higher than another, but that those who teach must be servants, washing one another from the dust and dirt of this world at the feet of others.

By Yahweh and His Spirit/*Ruah* through Yeshua, we are made clean, but as long as we walk this Earth, we come into contact with things that are not clean. The symbolism, the fullness of cleansing through His Spirit and the essence of His loving service as we serve one another in love through the washing of another's feet is said to be remembered.

We are to do this for one another. The physical repetition of this and its spiritual nature is heartening for both the giver and receiver.

We know a lot about the blood and the shed blood of Yeshua/Jesus for salvation. This is the other part—the part that appears to be the essence from God Himself in ways of His life-giving water.

The name Adam, broken down in Hebrew, is *Au* meaning "dust" and *dam*, meaning "blood." *Dam*=blood is the earthly component to our lives on earth. YHVH gathered the dust and breathed into Adam, and the waters of His breath (*Ruah*/spirit/breath) filled him.

A lot of our household dust comes from our skin. It dries and sluffs off as dust. But regarding our blood, it is life-giving on Earth. It is part of our earthly existence as in A-dam.

Yeshua came as Son of Man and YHVH, born of a virgin with the blood of life on Earth, perfected for our salvation as Savior to shed that blood as the payment of sin in our human existence.

> Every moving thing that lives shall be food for you, and as I gave you the green plants, I give you everything. 4 But you shall not eat flesh with its life that is, its blood. 5 And for your lifeblood I will require a reckoning; from every beast I will require it and from man. From his fellow man I will require a reckoning for the life of man. 6 "Whoever sheds the blood of man, by man his blood be shed, for God made man in his own image..." (Genesis 9:3-6 ESV)
>
> It is sown a natural body; it is raised a spiritual body. There is a natural body, and there is a spiritual body. 45And so it is written, The first man Adam was made a living soul; the last Adam was made a quickening spirit. 46However, that was not first which is spiritual, but that which is natural; and afterward that which is spiritual... (1 Corinthians 15:44-46)

This order of natural and physical representation in the Old Testament helps fortell the Spiritual life fulfilled through Christ. This connects the Old Testament to the New Testament. The physical and the spiritual overlap. The Bible reveals how to live a physical life spiritually through this sacred relationship.

Ask yourself how much you allow and notice the spiritual in your natural life. The more you live in the relationship with Yahweh through His Spirit/*Ruah*, the more you see the spiritual now.

Your gift of breath, words, prayers, and communion with your Creator opens life with eternal impact. He is as near as the breath within you, the rains that fall upon your head, the dew at your feet, the songs within the breath of the birds, the life all around you.

Yet not everything is seen. Just as electrons, protons and neutrons make up an atom, we can't see the electrons, but we know they are there. "The wind blows wherever it pleases. You hear its sound, but you cannot tell where it comes from or where it is going. So it is with everyone born of the Spirit." (John 3:8)

As the waters separated from the waters and Creation began from the Word of YHVH, in the beginning was the Word and the Word was with God and the Word was God. Yeshua came as the Living Word.

Remembering the tie in Leviticus of the clay jar filled with water, the scarlet thread, the blood of the one dove and the live dove set free, the cedar and the hyssop. It all ties to Yeshua and His death and resurrection and its meaning for us. This portion of Scripture in Hebrews will now stand out to you boldly and more beautiful.

> For when Moses had spoken every precept to all the people according to the law, he took the blood of calves and of goats, with water, and scarlet wool, and hyssop, and sprinkled both the book, and all the people, saying, "This is the blood of the testament which God has enjoined to you." (Hebrews 9:19-20)

The first miracle Moses performed through the power of God was turning water (the Nile) into blood in the Old Testament. Yeshua, coming from heaven not by water only, but by blood and water, is indicating that He is now man with blood in Him. The water turning into blood into water brought death to the fish and all living things in the water. The miracle/plague was to lead Pharoa to set God's people free. Yeshua bled with His own blood to free us from sin.

Yeshua's first miracle in the New Testament is turning the water into a new wine at the wedding in Cana.

> 6 Nearby stood six stone water jars, the kind used by the Jews for ceremonial washing, each holding from twenty to thirty gallons.

7 Yeshua said to the servants, "Fill the jars with water"; so they filled them to the brim.

8 Then he told them, "Now draw some out and take it to the master of the banquet."

They did so, 9 and the master of the banquet tasted the water that had been turned into wine. He did not realize where it had come from, though the servants who had drawn the water knew. Then he called the bridegroom aside 10 and said, "Everyone brings out the choice wine first and then the cheaper wine after the guests have had too much to drink; but you have saved the best till now." (John 2:6-11)

As Yeshua gave the disciples wine the night before his crucifixion, he said, "This is my blood of the covenant, which is poured out for many for the forgiveness of sins." (Matthew 26:28)

YHVH had saved the best till now. This wine, the blood made perfect and drinkable, the best saved till now is one to bring a life enjoyed and celebrated. Not into drunkenness, but a purified drink of a wedding celebration. The blood of Yeshua is the blood that set us free from the bondage of sin. Purified, we are set free we come into communion with Him.

The Spirit and the Bride say, "Come." And let the one who hears say, "Come." And let the one who is thirsty come; let the one who desires take the water of life without price. (Revelation 22:17)

"Binding his foal to the vine and his donkey's colt to the choice vine, he has washed his garments in wine and his vesture in the blood of grapes." (Genesis 49:11)

Yeshua will return again as the Bridegroom for His Bride and there will be a great banquet.

And I heard as it were the voice of a great multitude, and as the voice of many waters, and as the voice of mighty thunder, saying, Alleluia: for the Lord God omnipotent reigns. 7 Let us be glad and rejoice, and give honor to him: for the marriage of the Lamb is come, and his wife has made herself ready. 8 And to her was granted that she should be arrayed in fine linen, clean and white: for the fine linen is the righteousness of saints... (Revelation 19:6-7)

I would like to share a passage from *Hebrews for Christians* that was posted on their Facebook page:

"The fear of the LORD God is called yirat ha'shamayim, or yirat Hashem (יִרְאַת יהוה). This is not a superstitious dread of divine retribution as much as a sense of honor, respect, reverence, and awe over apprehending the power and "weight" of the sacredness of the miracle of life... We fear the LORD when we become awake, when our blind eyes are opened, and we then realize that our lives are a gift, a wonder, a divine possibility, and therefore a great responsibility. We have a holy ambivalence, a fearful hope, as we rejoice with trembling, since we understand that the Divine Presence is involved with all that we say, do, and think... Like Jacob we exclaim, מַה־נּוֹרָא הַמָּקוֹם / "How awesome is this place!" (Gen. 28:17)"

Here's an excerpt from *An Experience in Israel,* by David Housholder:

***"Here I stand**, bare feet on ancient stone. Looking down at the water...*

How did I get here?

It's 3am in Tsfat, Israel. Dark outside. Full moon over the 4,000 year-old graveyard behind me...

I was on the way home to California from a business trip in London.

As if by an unseen hand, I was led out of my well-worn hotel room and down the switchbacks to this holiest of places in this holiest of cities. Yitzak Luria's Mikveh.

I feel like Indiana Jones, except there is no khaki or wide-brimmed hat...I am as naked as the day I was born, no barrier, coram Deo. Even my watch and wedding ring have been taken off.

Just me. Just God. Just now.

My name, David, which never made much sense to me, seems oddly right for, perhaps, the first time ever. I have cultivated nicknames all my life. I think of the double delta of David's monogram...

I think back over the last 48 hours here in Galilee.

Invited into the back rooms of synagogues...

Rabbis pointing through the texts of "secret books" in Hebrew and asking questions....

- How did you learn Hebrew?
- Your name is David, are you sure you aren't Jewish? You look Russian...
- Where do you sense the presence of God here in Tsfat? Where is that feeling the strongest?
- What are you doing here?

I did not choose to stand here. I'm not even sure what a mikveh is…I was led here…

I need answers to three questions. Just two days ago, I wrote those questions on a tiny slip of paper, rolled it up, and placed it in the Western Wall of the temple mount in Jerusalem at sunrise. My forehead against the cool ancient stone, my palms up high, time collapsed…the better part of an hour evaporated like the morning fog…

It is dark outside. Not even the roosters have begun to crow…

I slide into the biting cold of the fresh spring water, holding the pole and stepping down the ancient steps. I breathe deeply and submerge….

The world disappears.

I pull my knees up against my chest, going fetal in this womb-tomb.

An avid surfer, I am used to being underwater and I gently roll backwards….

A glow emanates from nowhere and everywhere. I open my eyes underwater to confirm the experience and the light vanishes…

I come up for air twice and submerge again. The glow returns, and I feel enveloped in the Khesed-love of the Creator. Answers come to me faster than I can receive them.

I generate a will to receive.

Something shifts around me. The third time under turns into a dream. I feel as if I am breathing underwater. The glow gets warm.

All of my theological legalisms about baptism vanish and dissolve into an ocean of God's presence.

As I climb out and dry off, my soul comes to total rest. I will walk for hours until the hilltop town awakens. Like an old snakeskin, I have shed something. A new season is starting…

Where is your "mikveh" where you take off everything in the presence of God?

When's the last time you were there....?"

May you see YHVH in all things, may you know Him and know you are made with divine love and that your life has great purpose. Your life is for so much more. Draw near to Him, and He will draw near to you.

This is he that came by water and blood, even Yeshua Christ; not by water only, but by water and blood. And it is the Spirit /Ruah that bears witness, because the Spirit/Ruah is truth. 7For there are three that bear record in heaven, the Father, the Word, and the Holy Ghost/ Ruah Ha Kodesh: and these three are one. 8 And there are three that bear witness in earth, the Spirit/Ruah, and the water, and the blood: and these three agree in one. (1 John 5:6-8)

He saved us, not because of righteous things we had done, but because of his mercy. He saved us through the washing of rebirth and renewal by the Holy Spirit, whom he poured out on us generously through Yeshua the Christ our Savior, so that being justified by his grace we might become heirs according to the hope of eternal life. (Titus 3:5-7)

When my father-in-law was nearing the end of his life, his faith grew the most in that time. He received so many words of love, and his life was extended through that. He even managed to share back with us his words of love for us.

His last words to me in a struggle of quiet whisper and great effort were, "Tell them all about Jesus. Jesus. Jesus. Jesus."

His inhales became shorter and his exhales longer as he neared physical death. On hospice information sites, it says that the final breath is an exhale.

Yahweh's design for our last breath is intentionally an exhale. In my research of what the last breath is, the only time it may not be an exhale upon death is when one is hung or strangled.

YHVH's reverence for breath as well as for blood is found in Acts 15:20: "But that we write to them, that they abstain from pollutions of idols, and from fornication, and from things strangled, and from blood."

As man continues to search for water and life the sciences prove more about it. In July 2011, scientists found the largest mass of water ever discovered. It is 30 billion trillion miles away in a quasar named APM 08279+5255. The water measures at least 140 trillion times the water in all our oceans.

The image astoundingly resembles a cross.

(Image Credit: NASA/ESA)

"He has made everything beautiful in its time. He has also set eternity in the human heart; yet no one can fathom what YHVH has done from beginning to end." (Ecclesiastes 3:11)

10 Whoever desires to love life and see good days, let him keep his tongue from evil and his lips from speaking deceit; 11 let him turn away from evil and do good; let him seek peace and pursue it. 12 For the eyes of YHVH are on the righteous, and his ears are open to their prayer. But the face of YHVH is against those who do evil.

13 Now who is there to harm you if you are zealous for what is good? 14 But even if you should suffer for righteousness' sake, you will be blessed. Have no fear of them, nor be troubled, 15 but in your hearts honor Christ the Lord as holy, always being prepared to make a defense to anyone who asks you for a reason for the hope that is in you; yet do it with gentleness and respect, 16 having a good conscience, so that, when you are slandered, those who revile your good behavior in Christ may be put to shame. 17 For it is better to suffer for doing good, if that should be God's will, than for doing evil.

18 For Christ also suffered once for sins, the righteous for the unrighteous, that he might bring us to God, being put to death in the flesh but made alive in the spirit, 19 in which he went and proclaimed to the spirits in prison, 20 because they formerly did not obey, when God's patience waited in the days of Noah, while the ark was being prepared, in which a few, that is, eight persons, were brought safely through water. 21 Baptism, which corresponds to this, now saves you, not as a removal of dirt from the body but as an appeal to God for a good conscience, through the resurrection of Jesus Christ, 22 who has gone into heaven and is at the right hand of God, with angels,

authorities, and powers having been subjected to him. (1 Peter 3:10-22 ESV)

For the Lord Himself will descend from heaven with a shout, with the voice of the archangel and with the trumpet of God, and the dead in Christ will rise first. 17 Then we who are alive and remain will be caught up together with them in the clouds to meet the Lord in the air, and so we shall always be with the Lord. 18 Therefore comfort one another with these words. (1 Thessalonians 4:16-18)

I'm using the NAS translation of Revelation 1:7-8 because of the capitalization it uses for emphasis.

BEHOLD, HE IS COMING WITH THE CLOUDS, and every eye will see Him, even those who pierced Him; and all the tribes of the earth will mourn over Him. So it is to be. Amen. 8 "I am the Alpha and the Omega," says YHVH, "who is and who was and who is to come, the Almighty." (Revelation 1:7-8)

It is the Spirit who gives life; the flesh is no help at all. The words that I have spoken to you are spirit and life. (John 6:63)

It was nearing the end of my vacation along the shores of the Gulf of Mexico. I looked out at that beautiful expanse of turquoise water, and I ached. I did not want to leave it. YHVH spoke and said to me, "You are not leaving it; it is a part of you. You take it everywhere you go. Look at My greater creation." And I looked.

There were people.

People along the shores.

The young and old, couples, families, and individuals were walking along the water or in it. There were people swimming and surfing in it.

There were people in boats upon it moving quickly, and some had stopped and were fishing. There were people riding parasails, floating quietly high above on the breezes.

I saw them.

I saw the greater creation of man in YHVH's image by His love.

Your heart has eternity set in it.

ACKNOWLEDGMENTS

I'd like to thank David Housholder and Rolf Garborg for your professional advice as authors and Bible scholars and for each of your inspiring ministries and teachings. I'd like to also thank Graham Cooke. The three of you modeled what it is like to write in freedom and in truth, stepping away from the confines of religious formality and speaking from the heart. It is an honor to be allowed to include portions of your inspirations in *Sacred Breath*.

Mom and Dad, thank you for listening to me with each fresh revelation I excitedly ran to you with and for your insights and prayers along the way.

To my children, you each have given me my greatest appreciation for life, and I love you. Sam, your growing up years by my side through so many experiences in this book have been remarkable. Thank you for leaning in next to me and watching while I typed up the last pages.

My gratitude also goes to Emmaus Lutheran Church in Bloomington, MN, The Blessing House in Victoria, MN, and Good Word Ministries in Durham, England for providing my first ministry opportunities to come and speak on the lessons within *Sacred Breath*.

To Raymond Muckuk, Seth Yazzie, Darla Provancial, Pastor Titus Upham, and Pastor Tom Valtierra: your miraculous timing of showing up for me when I needed a word of encouragement to confirm the work and press me to get this done is why it's here now. You are led by the Spirit. Collectively as Indigenous People, this is powerful. You are the ones who have called this forth and helped pray it through. To YHVH be the glory!

ABOUT THE AUTHOR

Lori Paul is an ex-minivan-driving soccer mom who got called out of the suburban wilderness and into the adventure of her life. Obeying the voice of the Holy Spirit, she is the author of *A Warrior's Circle of Yesterday, Today and Tomorrow*.

Her desire to serve the heart of Yahweh led her to places like Mt. Kilimanjaro, Reservations in the US and Canada, and a 2.5-year communications director position for Breaking Free, an anti-sex trafficking organization. Lori became a fearless voice for the voiceless, testified on two bills that became laws, and called for the activation of a Missing and Murdered Indigenous Women Taskforce.

She speaks and writes on topics from Scripture to the darkest places of mankind and has spoken in France, England, Tanzania, Canada, and across the United States from Washington DC to Washington State. It's a good thing she loves to travel and camp.

You can find Lori online at Truthwalker.org

→ Canon Trump
   Osyop

New Water
Toilet to tap

Plan Retreat — Corn
Board Line —
Coast Line under attack

— Earth Ink —

What are they spraying
Why

Pre industrial   Disable up
                       Table top
(Dark Sister) Biology * mineralizing
2001   our water